WHAT PEOPLE ARE SAYING ABOUT THIS BOOK

I couldn't put the book down. I was so intrigued and pulled into each of these stories, crying and laughing with each person who shared their life experience as if I was going through it with them. My faith has definitely been strengthened and this has led me to pray for and be aware of God's presence in my life. Faith is believing without seeing, yet these real-life experiences give us a clear glimpse into the love and power of God and how He transforms us.

No matter where we are in our life journey, these stories demonstrate time after time that there is nothing God can't do and can't change if we just cry out to Him. I personally experience a lot of hurt and fear and shame. As with many in this book, I, too, have built up walls around me so that I won't get hurt or be judged. This book encouraged me to reach out to God and seek His help.

At one point while reading the book, I found myself falling to my knees and praying to the Lord to release me from my bondage and give me the ability to forgive and love. As a result, my life has been deeply impacted! God bless Kathleen and Anh for sharing such inspirational stories with us!

Vera Wang

Co-Founder, Miss Fashion Week

Founder/CEO, Viviona Fashion Manufacturing and Branding
Managing Partner, F8 Marketing Lab

This book on testimonials shows how God's love and grace is not just theological, but is real and transformational. These varied and dramatic real life stories display how God takes us just as we are despite our shame, deception, past, sin, or wounds. Need an encouragement of your faith, then read this book!

Brad Dacus

President Pacific Justice Institute

Faithfulness - that's the first word that comes to my mind when reading this book by Anh and Kathleen Le. God is forever faithful in hearing the cries of His people. In this special book about testimonies of people from varied walks of life, it shows that God always shows up whenever there is a crisis in our life, if we will just call on Him. Story after story reveals how despair and hopelessness can drive men and women to involve themselves in life styles and actions they never thought would happen to them. But, through God sending the right people at the right time to minister to them, they have come through some pretty horrific circumstances.

Thank you to Anh and Kathleen for giving us the insight into everyday people who have struggled, but have an ever-faithful God who is standing at the door ready to help, just like He did in your lives. Also, thank you for your testimonies and what God has done and is continuing to do through your ministry. I would recommend this book to anyone and everyone as a source of encouragement that will lead to an understanding of what God has done for each person mentioned in this book. What God did for them, He can do for you! Don't Give Up!

Keith L Ivester

Administrative Bishop

Florida Church of God State Office

EVIDENCE
Real Life Stories of People Who Encountered God

© 2017 Awakening The Nations

ISBN-10: 0-9991012-0-X

ISBN-13: 978-0-9991012-0-9

Published by Awakening The Nations – Anh and Kathleen Le
Orlando, Florida, USA

All rights reserved. This book or any portion thereof may not be reproduced or trans-mitted in any form or used in any manner whatsoever including electronic or mechanical, photocopying, and recording without the express written permission of the publisher except for the use of brief quotations in a book review. Requests for permission should be addressed in writing by visiting www.awakeningthenations.com

All Scripture quotations, unless otherwise indicated, are taken from THE HOLY BI-BLE Scriptures marked NKJV are taken from the NEW KING JAMES VERSION (NKJV): Scripture taken from the NEW KING JAMES VERSION®. Copyright© 1982 by Thomas Nelson, Inc. Used by permission. All rights reserved.

Scriptures marked NIV are taken from the NEW INTERNATIONAL VERSION (NIV):

Scripture taken from THE HOLY BIBLE, NEW INTERNATIONAL VERSION ®. Copyright© 1973, 1978, 1984, 2011 by Biblica, Inc.™. Used by permission of Zondervan

Cover design by Nicole Phillip - Ministry Event Marketing
www.ministryeventmarketing.com

Edited by Julie Baker & Make This Matter, LLC

Stock or custom editions of Awakening the Nations Publishing titles may be pur-chased in bulk for educational, business, ministry, fundraising, or sales promotional use. For information, please e-mail kle@awakeningthenations.com

All of the stories written in this book are based on true events and people, some of the names and a few of the details of the stories have been left out to protect the privacy of the individuals.

Printed in the United States of America.

11 12 13 14 15 16 7 6 5 4 3 2 1

CONTENTS

Foreword by Joe Battaglia ix

Introduction xi

1. My Life Is A Wreck! 1
2. Atheist To Jesus 11
3. Running From God 19
4. Deception 27
5. Skeletons In The Closet 37
6. Shattered Dreams 45
7. Stolen Childhood 51
8. New Age & Confused 59
9. Sexually Assaulted 69
10. Angry And Abusive 75
11. Life After Abortion 85
12. Witchcraft's Deception 93
13. Life After Death 101
14. Help With Anxiety & Depression 109
15. Conclusion 113
16. Additional Information And Resources 115

FOREWORD

There's a story in Scripture in the Gospel of Luke where John the Baptist's disciples come to Jesus and ask him this question: "Are you the Messiah we've been expecting, or should we keep looking for someone else?"

Now, that seems like a strange question to come from John, since it was he who baptized Jesus and heard God's voice from heaven say that He was well pleased with Jesus. And also in light of the miracles that Jesus had been doing. So, it would have been understandable for Jesus to say something like, "Hey disciples are you kidding! Tell John to get with the program!"

No, Jesus doesn't say that. Instead he says this: "Go back to John and report what you have seen and heard: The blind receive sight, the lame walk, those who have leprosy are cured, the deaf hear, the dead are raised, and the good news is preached to the poor" (Luke 7:20).

Jesus could have been describing Kathleen and Anh Le, the authors of this book, who have assembled an inspiring anthology of modern day miracles of redemption. The Le's are living proof of God's power to redeem lives, and through their storytelling, draw a startling parallel to Jesus' words in Luke and to the other stories in the book that pose these questions:

- Is anyone more blind than someone that refuses to see his or her pain and continue to languish in persistent despair?
- Is there anyone more lame than someone unable to walk with integrity?
- Is there anyone more leprous than a young girl who sells herself into prostitution to support a drug habit or gets caught in the web of human trafficking?

- Is there anyone more deaf than someone who refuses to hear his or her heart crying out for God?
- Is there anyone more dead than someone hooked on drugs and who's lost their mind to this insidious addiction?
- And is there anyone poorer than someone who tries to fill his or her life with riches, and yet lives in a perennial poverty of the spirit?

Like John's disciples, people are still asking that question of Jesus. And the answer is still the same. Jesus is the same yesterday, today, and forever.

With personal insights into their own lives and the people they feature, accented with Biblical reflections, Kathleen and Anh have written a book to encourage anyone looking for the answer that John the Baptist's disciples asked! Jesus still says to us the same thing he said back then: Go and report what you have seen and heard.

The Le's have done just that.

Pick up this book if you need to be reminded that God still trans-forms lives!

Joe Battaglia
Author, Broadcaster
President of Renaissance Communications

EVIDENCE
Real Life Stories of People Who Encountered God

INTRODUCTION FROM KATHLEEN LE

Have you ever wondered is God even real? Many have this question because they have never experienced God and if they did, would they recognize it? Others question God's existence because of all the bad things that happen in this world. If God was real, why did He allow this to happen, why is there so much evil, how could he love me, one out of billions of people? I too had many of these questions. I felt so small compared to the universe and wondered if God is real. He probably didn't even notice me and if he did, He probably hated me. I felt so small in the big scheme of things. Many nights I wondered who am I, what am I doing this for, and what is my purpose? If God isn't real and there isn't life after death, what is the point? Why would we spend so many years building memories and friendships just to have it all end after death? All of those questions were answered after having my own encounter with God.

My husband, Anh, is a former atheist and has a Molecular Cellular Developmental Biology degree. He hated Christians and tried to disprove God through science. After he had his own personal encounter with God, he now sees that science supports the belief in God. When we got married, we began to meet people who had similar stories about encountering God. We were so intrigued to hear how these people with extremely different backgrounds also found evidence for God. Our findings, if there were a spiritual scientific study, could prove God's existence. We started a radio show in 2015 and have already interviewed over 400 people from all walks of life who encountered God... former prostitutes, homeless men and women, victims of violence and abuse, drug addicts, pro athletes, those into witchcraft, and many suffering the effects of stress and anxiety.

We have included our personal stories, along with 11 people who have been guests on our radio show, encompassing a variety of life experiences and trials you or someone you know might be facing, to bring encouragement to readers. The stories compiled in this book have nothing in common except one thing: Although they didn't believe in God or turned away from Him, they are all people with real problems who found answers in a real God.

Our desire is that you will not only be inspired by each of these stories, but regardless of what you are going through, you will find hope in this book and that you too will have a God encounter!

Each chapter begins by posing a question and short introduction from Kathleen, followed by the Life Changing Story as is recited by each person in his or her own words. After each personal story, Anh shares Insights, Points to Ponder, and an amazing Prayer to Encounter God.

We will begin our journey by sharing the personal circumstances that forever changed our lives.

MY LIFE IS A WRECK!

Evidence that God Can Help People with PTSD, Bipolar, and Severe Depression

Kathleen Le's Story

I was told the true story of a woman who had an affair with a married man and became pregnant. In her mind, the only solution was to abort the baby, thus, not having to face the shame and ridicule it would bring to both families.

She decided to have an abortion. However, when her neighbor caught wind of this, and brought to her a picture of her three children and placed a black mark near them. She said, "If you abort this child, you will forever hold in your heart a black hole that will follow you the rest of your life."

As a result, the woman decided not to abort that child.

That child in her womb was me.

How grateful I am to have been given a chance to live!

My birth father had three children from his marriage, and my mom had three from hers. I always felt like the odd duckling. Although my father made promises to me that he would see me on my birthday or at a holiday, he basically abandoned me. I've only been with him a hand-full of times in my entire life. Oh, how I desired to have my dad in my life! I felt so unwanted and believed that I was a big mistake.

Knowing I was almost aborted and that I came from an adulteress affair kept me thinking I was just a big accident.

As a single mom, my mother was working two to three jobs at a time, trying to keep a roof over our heads; and, since she was always away working, we were left alone to fend for ourselves. I can still remember the hunger pangs I had on a constant basis. We never had food in the house, so I became the proverbial latch-key kid. At night I would often cry myself to sleep, wishing I had a mommy or daddy at home to tuck me in. Mom had a hard upbringing herself and tried to deal with her own pain by self-medicating. She was addicted to marijuana and constantly entered into and out of relationships. Having parties at our house wasn't uncommon and my birthdays ended up becoming another reason for the adults to party.

Our home had no boundaries, rules, or expectations. Well, actually there was one rule. Mom told me she didn't care what I did as long as I told her where I was.

So, at age 13, I was running around with the wrong crowd and was actually allowed entrance into a Mexican nightclub, which was a bar! Every Thursday night to Sunday night, this is where I would be. If I made it to class on Fridays and Mondays, I was very late.

From age 13, in the 7th grade, to age 19, I was associated with one of the toughest gangs that originated from California and most moved to Colorado to escape police. During this time, I was involved in a drive-by shooting, a house shooting, and was spared from being shot 5 times. The fist fights were constant with other girls. Many times I had to run to escape being assaulted. At 15 years old, I lost my virginity to a date rape. I never felt the same after and struggled with knowing what was true love.

I began to suffer panic attacks because I felt so unloved and rejected. I believed there was no hope for me, and at times I just wanted to die. Anti-depressants were prescribed for me, but they only numbed my emotions.

Hoping that I would at least graduate from high school after going to 18 schools, I was placed in an alternative school. At least I would graduate from high school, even if it was a year late. During this time, I discovered that my boyfriend, whom I idolized, was cheating on me. As if that wasn't bad enough, he told me that if I left him, he would kill himself. I felt trapped, alone, and even more hopeless. All I could do was think about dying. I had only three months left to finish high school, but instead, I laid in bed for days battling depression.

I finally said, "God if you are real… kill me or show me a sign." Moments later the home phone rang, and it was one of my High School teachers. She said, "Kathleen, this is your teacher, Mrs. C. I haven't seen you at school. When are you coming back?"

I said "Mrs. C, I quit… I can't take life anymore and I don't want to finish school."

She said, "Kathleen, I along with other teachers have elected you to be the Valedictorian of this class—you can't quit now!" I was so surprised that they would consider me. However, that was not enough incentive for me to continue on. Then Mrs. C said, "Kathleen, can I pray for you?"

I thought, "I grew up believing there was a God and after all I just did ask for a sign." I allowed her to pray with me and felt some sense of peace. Looking back, I am amazed that this public-school teacher risked her entire career for me. She told me that if I came back to school, she would pray with me daily. I did return, and almost on a daily basis, we would retreat to the maintenance room closet to pray, because we knew it wasn't safe to pray openly.

She began pouring the truth of God's Word into my heart. One day I finally prayed the 'sinner's prayer' with her and asked Jesus into my life.

Even though I had made a huge step in the right direction, I was not totally committed to God. At that time, I didn't understand what it was to have a relationship with God. I was trying to fix myself. I was still hanging around people who were doing terrible things—very dangerous things-- but I just couldn't separate myself from them. I was looking for love in all the wrong places, as the song goes!

I dated every kind of guy, thinking that at some point that I would finally find the right one and all would be fine in my world. I hoped to meet a good-looking guy who was a Christian. I would meet guys who weren't Christians and tried to convert them. Unfortunately, that never seemed to work, the baggage I was carrying was only getting heavier as I searched for love. I was still empty and miserable.

In an attempt to earn the attention and respect of my father, I enrolled in broadcast school and eventually became a television reporter. Surely THAT would win him over! I somehow thought that he would finally see me as his own and be proud of me. Sadly, it did not happen the way I imagined. Although he seemed proud and accepting, there was still something missing. All of the expectations I had of finally being happy because I was now an important television reporter and had turned my life around evaporated. It also confused me that every relationship I formed with a man and every career success always ended with me feeling even more rejected and extremely unfulfilled.

One night I went on a date with a guy to a "Hell House," a haunted house created by a local church every year. As we waited in line, I heard a song I had never heard before, "I am waiting for you, wait for me too" by Rebecca Saint James. I immediately realized that the man I was dating was not going to be my husband. Somehow, I felt there was actually someone who might BE waiting for me. But, I was delaying it by trying to find love on my own. That Hell House was a real wake-up call for me. There were three ways to exit from the haunted house: Hell, Heaven, or Unknown. I didn't know where I was going, but not wanting to embarrass myself, I chose Heaven. Realizing this guy was not going to be my husband made it easy to walk away from the relationship. Although I called myself a Christian, the truth was, my life was full of hypocrisy. With a deep conviction and desire to be an example to my nieces and nephews, I gave up partying and dating. Shortly after, church became my new thing.

At about the same time I began to seek the Lord, I met Anh. One of our first dates was at a Campus Crusade for Christ Rally. That was a 180 from the activities I had always attended! From there, our relationship blossomed. Early on, it was apparent that Anh was different from anyone else I had ever dated. For starters, he did not expect me to give him anything in return. That was so opposite of what I was used to. In fact, we had not even kissed yet when he proposed and gave me my engagement ring! Our first kiss was at our wedding ceremony.

At age 31 I was happily married with two children, being well-provided for by my loving husband, but I was diagnosed with Post Traumatic Stress Disorder, bi-polar disorder, and severe depression. As a stay-at-home mom, I had plenty of time to think about my past mistakes. All I could think about was, "If only I never hung around that gang… if only I had a mom and dad around as a kid… if only…."

I harbored so much fear, anxiety, anger, and regret. I was so uncertain if God even loved me. Though we had a ministry and we were helping others, it seemed like nothing was helping me. I thought, "maybe God only loves Pastors, really good people, and my husband who just seems to be almost perfect." Even the Women's Bible study group I was part of didn't seem to have the answers either. They were all on anti-depressants and rather than believing God could heal me, they began advising me on the best drug to take. It was at that Bible study that I felt all hope was lost. I thought to myself, "If God isn't able to help me, then no one is."

Anti-depressants weren't an option for me since I had taken them for years and found they never worked. Though I tried everything to find peace and wholeness, nothing worked. I went to doctors and counselors, tried special diets and researched self-help methods. I had tried it all and felt like a prisoner in my own body. Looking back, it's easy to see that fixing a spiritual problem by physical means never works.

Because I feared I would be admitted to a mental hospital, I kept these deepest thoughts to myself. Most couldn't understand how a girl who has everything could be so miserable, especially considering where I came from. The severe torment of the last bout of depression lasted for eight long months. I couldn't sleep and was barely functioning. My thinking was that death would be better than being stuck in some mental hospital for the rest of my life.

I kept hearing in my mind, "You aren't worth anything. You're a failure. Why not just kill yourself? You're just a big mistake and everyone would be better off without you. There is no other way out."

After continuously being beaten down with these uncontrollable thoughts, my only way to alleviate this pain would be to end it. Though I knew suicide was selfish, it seemed like the only option.

In the depths of my own hell, I would give God one more chance to help me. My thoughts were hopeless: "He probably doesn't even see me. I'm just one person out of seven billion people. I shouldn't have even been born as far as He is concerned." In desperation and with no other options left, I did what I should've done years ago. I cried out with all I had in me—a cry of helpless surrender. "JESUS, DO YOU LOVE ME?!" Tears were flowing from my sleepless eyes and I yelled once again with everything in me, "JESUS DO YOU EVEN LOVE ME?!" To my surprise, a vision of red letters appeared in my eyes, one at a time. What was happening? I don't even believe in visions. The big red letters came together and flashed inside of my closed eyes: "LOVE, LOVE, YOU."

I was shocked and amazed that the God of the universe would reach down to me in my deepest, darkest pit and show me His Love. Any doubt of God not being real went right out the window. "Jesus, how do I live with this torment and PTSD?" I distinctly heard Him say, "Fight back! Resist the Devil and he will flee!" I now know that this is a scripture verse found in James 4:7.

For three whole days, I fought. I literally kicked and punched and kept shouting, "Go! In Jesus' name!" I must've looked silly to my family, but I didn't care. I was desperate for freedom. I read the Bible and spoke the scriptures out loud continuously.

Suddenly, I was FREE!!! The Bible tells us that the "Truth will set you free." Jesus IS the Truth!

Since that time, I have never had a panic attack, suffered anxiety or depression, or been suicidal. In fact, all PTSD, bi-polar, and depression left me and now I have a new way of thinking. It is a continual fight as I now know that I'm dealing with a spiritual realm.

A man of God - Todd White - whom I had never heard of, was speaking at a conference only weeks after my encounter with God. I'll never forget what he said. He looked in my direction and said, "You are not a mistake!" How did he know that I believed that lie for almost my entire life? When that truth came to me, it was like an arrow straight to my heart. All of the lies I had believed were crushed and I immediately understood that God does not make mistakes. Humans might make mistakes, but God never makes mistakes. He created us and formed and fashioned each one of us in our mother's womb (Psalm 139). Jesus has a plan and purpose for every single person on this earth! We just can't give up!

An amazing thing happened. The Lord allowed me the privilege of leading my dad to Jesus just before he died. Later, I had beautiful dream of seeing my dad in Heaven worshipping the Lord. My mom also received Jesus and is serving the Lord faithfully.

Insights with Anh

According to the American Foundation for Suicide Prevention, suicide claims more lives than war, murder, and natural disasters combined. In 2015, suicide was the second leading cause of death for adults between the ages of 10 and 34 years in the United States. Over 50 percent of all people who die by suicide suffer from major depression. If one includes alcoholics who are depressed, this figure rises to over 75 percent. The problem with depression is that many people who struggle, like Kathleen did, never get help. People tend to isolate and feel alone. Many fear what others will think or they fear being put in a mental hospital. Kathleen was afraid of sharing her thoughts and feelings with me because she feared that I would reject her, not understand, think she was crazy, and throw her into a mental hospital. Having a person you feel safe to share your feelings with is so important. Knowing that you are not crazy is also helpful. Many people have weird thoughts once and a while, but they probably won't share that with anyone.

When Kathleen and I realized her problem was more than just a medical issue and that she was dealing with a spiritual issue, we changed our approach. We began to pray, fight back by using the word of God, the Bible, replacing the old cycle of thoughts with new ones. Kathleen would have a thought and I would help her to break the negative cycle of thinking about the thought by saying "so what". Let me give you an example. We learned that fear leads to anxiety and anxiety leads to depression. Proverbs 12:25 says "Anxiety in the heart of man causes depression, but a good word makes it glad." If we don't answer the thought and replace it with a good thought, then it will remain.

So Kathleen would share a fear or bad thought. I would say to her, "What if that happened?" She would respond with another concern or fear-filled comment and then I would say, "And what if that happened?" We would go fully through the worst case scenario of the situations and her concerns got weaker. She began to respond, "So what if that happens? God will help me.. So, what if that happens? I will be in Heaven." She began to use scripture as a replacement of the old thoughts. You see the things we think are so vital that the Bible says, "As a man thinks in his heart, so is he" (Proverbs 23:7).

We need to stop allowing the lies from the past to hold us from our today and our future. I have been called many names growing up. The things people said really did hurt, but I can't allow what others have said to determine my destiny.

If you can identify with this story, we have created a section at the back of this book with 14 practical things you can do to help with anxiety and depression.

Points to Ponder

1. Have you ever struggled with anxiety or depression?
2. What do you do when you feel alone?
3. How can the things you learned from this chapter help you in your own life?

Prayer to Encounter God

Lord, I pray for those who are reading this to understand just how much you love them. For those who are struggling with fear, anxiety, worry, depression, and suicidal desires, I break it off them now in the Mighty Name of Jesus. I command all fear, anxiety, worry, depression, and suicidal desires to leave right now, in Jesus name. I pray for Peace, Love, Joy, and Hope to fill those reading this. I thank You Lord that today is a new day and your mercies are new for all of us. Lord, we ask that you would guide us in all we do. We thank you Lord for setting us free from all those things that have held us captive. Amen

ATHEIST TO JESUS

Evidence that God Can Change the Mind of an Atheist

Anh Le's Story

My dad was Buddhist and my mother Catholic.

From the time I was very young, my father would insist that I "do meditation" with him. On the outside, I looked as if I was quietly meditating next to him, but usually I was thinking about Transformers or what I would do when allowed to go outside and play!

To me, there was a drabness about this that permeated our house. I felt it was a false peace. My father suffered from anxiety and was diagnosed as bi-polar, so for him, this was a way to keep him calm and help him cope.

When I was 12, and home alone one day, my dad came home from work early and asked me to sit down. "I'm leaving. Your mother and I are going to get a divorce."

I froze. This couldn't be true. In the Asian community, boys are raised to show no emotion. It would bring shame on the family. But, as he began walking to the door, I couldn't contain my emotions and began sobbing uncontrollably. He walked back and told me that everything would work out, that this was best for everyone, and it would make everyone happier. Then he walked out the door.

The first time that my mother learned of his departure was when she came home from work that afternoon. We were both in a state of shock.

Already conflicted because of the two different religions I had grown up with, I now decided there could not possibly be a God, since this was allowed to happen. Therefore, I decided I would be an atheist!

I had two goals for my life at this time: I wanted to be a doctor who made a lot of money, and I wanted to marry a beautiful blonde girl.

So, I made education my god. In college, I became a Molecular, Cellular, Developmental Biology Major, which would help me fulfil my goal of becoming a rich doctor. College also opened the door for drinking, using women, and spending countless nights at the dance clubs looking for girls. There were many hearts I broke as we would "fall in love," then I would move on to the next girl and break her heart.

I was really out of control by age 19. All of the goals and activities that I thought would bring me fulfillment, were making me miserable. I had absolutely no purpose in my life.

To me, religion was for the weak, those who need a crutch when they can't handle life. I was determined that I could make it on my own. After all, studying Evolution was a huge part of my education and it clearly reveals that it is the survival of the fittest. Strong people don't cry. They don't share feelings. It's a "survive or die" type of mentality.

I saw Christians as people who suffered a disease! I actually despised them. To me, they were just plain ignorant, displaying no logic. They so angered me that I became really good at using my logic to deconvert as many Christians as possible!

One night, I was driving home from a party feeling very depressed. All of the partying, drinking, and no purpose left me with a vacuum in my heart. I looked down at the Odometer, and part of it read 777, and it cheered me up a little bit because it was my lucky number. I looked up and over to the right saw I was passing a church. I distinctly heard a voice ask me, "Why don't you go to church?"

Of course, I ignored the question.

But, not too long after that, driving that same route, still very depressed, I looked down at the odometer and part of it again read 777. Once again, I heard that prompting to go to church; just one time. I looked up and there was that church again!

Even though I wasn't sure why, I pulled into the parking lot, entered the church and sat by myself in the last pew. The only church I knew expected total silence, so I bowed my head and stared at the floor. I pondered, "If God were even real, He wouldn't really care about me. He is probably doing His own thing. If He IS real, I will pay my respects, and then take my life. I want to quit this life, it isn't worth living."

I felt a hand on my shoulder and looked up. It was a man probably about the age of my own father. He asked if I was alone, and when I indicated I was, he invited me to sit with his family. A bit embarrassed, I followed and sat with them. As we began talking, it surfaced that his daughter attended the same college I did and was majoring in molecular biology. As it turned out, she was in one of my classes!

Looking around the church sanctuary, it suddenly dawned on me that there were many beautiful college-aged women attending! Wow! Perhaps church wasn't going to be such a downer after all! The church college group was having a weekend retreat, so they invited me to attend. Of course, all I could think about was scoring with any of these pretty girls! I had NO use for religion or the Bible.

Once I got to the retreat location and began to participate in the activities, I was both confused and a bit angry. These people were weird! The raunchy jokes I thought were hilarious just went over their heads, and the things they thought were funny bored me. But, did I mention there were a lot of pretty girls?

At one point, they asked each of us to take a Bible and find a quiet spot alone to search the Scriptures, study a portion, and share with the group. In true atheist fashion, I performed the "open book and point method." I did this many times, only to come to scriptures that made no sense to me, and seemed to allude to the judgment of God. I definitely didn't have any interest in that subject, so I would come back to the group with nothing to share.

Again, and again, that pastor was asking us to do this silly exercise, yet I couldn't bring myself to tell him I wasn't a Christian. On the last time, I was so frustrated, but I opened up the Bible anyway. To my astonishment, it opened to John 1:12, which reads "Yet to all who did receive him, to those who believed in his name, he gave the right to become children of God." Suddenly something clicked! I realized that to be a Christian, you didn't need to be some perfect person, but that you simply needed to receive and believe in Jesus. I looked up to heaven and said, "Well, Jesus if you are real, I receive you and believe in you."

When it was my turn to share, I just let the group have it. Finally, I would show those self-righteous Christians what I found in their Bible. In so many words I told them that they weren't so high and mighty having been born into Christianity. This verse said that ANYONE could receive Him if they believed in his name.

To my surprise, rather than igniting an argument, I looked around the circle to smiles and nods that said, "You finally get it!"

I still wanted to pick a fight. Later that night, I began arguing with one of the other guys and was just about ready to draw him into a fight. He lost his patience, and I got so angry, I resolved that I was just going to punch him. In the midst of clenching my fists, something extraordinary and rather supernatural happened. Time literally stood still between my raising my fist, and it was like everything around me had stopped. I heard a booming, thunderous voice say, "I know you." Then the thought came to my mind, "What would Jesus do?" Well, I knew for certain he would not throw a punch. To my amazement, while it had been a long time since I had known a father, I felt that I was loved and understood by a Father. THE Father, whose voice I had just heard.

Suddenly, I was zoomed back into time and all I could do was look to the heavens and quietly declare, "Jesus! You are real!" I vacillated between feeling I was going crazy to knowing that I had just experienced a supernatural revelation! Oddly enough, no one in that group thought there was anything out of the ordinary happening to me.

This prompted me to begin attending church regularly. The pastor recognized that I was a baby Christian and committed to disciple me, which helped me to learn and grow by leaps and bounds.

Some people wondered if I immediately got rid of my belief in evolution and become a creationist. Not so much; actually, I could not reconcile the theory of Evolution with the Bible teachings about God creating the earth. However, over time, as I began to look at the study of statistics, it became very apparent that theory of evolution was so unlikely, that believing in that theory made less sense than a loving God who created the world. This caused me to relook at everything I knew and believed before. God walked me through so much. It was revolutionary to how I understood how the world came to be.

Interestingly enough, even without much Bible study, the Holy Spirit began revealing to me right from wrong. I became so convicted about the many people I had hurt, that I went back to them and asked for forgiveness and reconciliation.

Another amazing miracle also happened when I totally surrendered my life to Christ. I was immediately set free from the anxiety and depression that I had experienced most of my life! One verse that sustained me during this transition was Matthew 6:25: "Therefore, I tell you, do not worry about your life, what you will eat or drink; or about your body, what you will wear. Is not life more than food, and the body more than clothes?" For the first time in 16 years, I was free from worry. This went totally against anything I had studied before about anxiety and depression, but there I was, totally set free by the power of Jesus.

As I searched the Scriptures and learned to pray, I learned how to hear the voice of God. He became a true Father to me. You see, I was head smart, but heart poor. I finally realized that without the direction and power of God's Holy Spirit, I could accomplish nothing.

In this new spiritual experience, I have also discovered the power of the Holy Spirit by literally being baptized into the Holy Spirit. When this happens, people are given a supernatural power to pray over people and see miracles happen! Sounds way out there right? I have been documenting the miracles of God and there are so many that I've lost count. I have prayed for a man in a coma, and he came out of it. I have prayed for people in wheelchairs and have seen them walk. I have prayed over demon-possessed people and seen them released from bondage. The reality of these things is so amazing, that I can't cease from studying the results of this phenomenon.

This is why I feel called to travel the world and share this message…to tell the truth about God, His Son Jesus, and the power of the Holy Spirit.

I know He is real. I know he can heal. I know he can save. And I know that if you will just believe, like me, you can walk in His spirit. I am walking evidence of the existence of God!

Insights with Anh

Do you struggle with the question "is God real?" I know many who wonder and even look to science for answers. But science has not yet caught up to what the Bible speaks about. Many thought science has already disproved the Bible, and has somehow contradicted it. Truthfully, science has only disproved folklore and wrong beliefs that religious people had, but it has not disproved the Bible. Jesus actually

RUNNING FROM GOD

Evidence that God can Touch a Homeless Drug Addict who had no Hope

Ricardo Malone became so desperate and fell to such a low point, that he actually resorted to eating out of trash cans. At times we can get pretty low in life with trials and tribulations. We feel like we've been beaten down to a point where we isolate ourselves or even turn away from the people who love us; or we even turn away from God. Many who go through trials say, "there is no God".

When we think about the Christian faith and being raised in a Christian home, we assume that a person who is raised with Christian values will grow up following all of the tenants of the Christian faith. We assume they will always live an obedient life, adhering to Biblical principles.

After becoming a believer in Jesus, I looked at Christian families and thought, "If only I would have grown up in a Christian home... then I never would've done the bad things I did." As I began to grow in my faith as a Christian, the Lord showed me that regardless of our upbringing, we all have a freewill and choose the path we want to walk—good or bad.

Those who grow up with Christianity need just as much forgiveness as those who grow up without it. The bad choices we make in life have consequences. I've spoken with many people who grew up in the church, but ended up going astray. Some felt so guilty for doing wrong that they steered clear from God and the church.

Is there hope for those who know what's right from wrong but still make bad choices? What about the ones who have been ensnared by doing wrongs/sins through temptation?

Ricardo Malone exemplifies for us how low one can go as he was at his breaking point.

~Kathleen

Ricardo Malone's Story

I was the oldest of eight children and raised in a loving, Christian home by a very godly mother. My future was bright. By age 19, I had married and landed a great job. I was even invited to join a vocal group and began traveling around the country singing. Positive experiences just seemed to come my way.

However, by age 20, things began to fall apart. It began with smoking marijuana and when the thrill of that wore off, I turned to other drugs and ended up sorely addicted to crack cocaine.

I quickly lost the trust of people. Because I failed a drug test at work, I lost the great job I had been blessed with. Eventually, my wife couldn't take it anymore and divorced me.

Sure, like many addicts, I went in for treatment time after time, and would do well for about 30 days. But then I would go right back to repeating my same destructive behavior over and over again. I had burned so many bridges in my hometown in Illinois that I had to move to Georgia. When things didn't get any better in Georgia, I packed up and moved to southern Florida.

I quickly discovered that running away from my problems did not make the problems go away. I was the problem. And wherever I went, the problem followed with me.

In southern Florida, I actually became involved in a church, which my brother pastored, thinking that would help; and it did for a short time. But sadly, I quickly returned to a life of drugs that eventually led me to living on the street, homeless.

My mother, who was such a wonderful lady, would have taken me in. It didn't matter to her what I had done. But I never wanted to go home until after the last time I was released from jail.

The crime that habitually sent me to jail over and over was shoplifting. But, that's the way I supported my habit. Every day I would go from store to store shoplifting, then sell those items on the street to support my habit. I might make on average $400-$500 a day selling the stuff I had stolen. But that was barely enough for the drugs. Many days I would only have $5 left to spend on food.

I was eating out of dumpsters. I'm not talking about just *looking* in a dumpster, I'm talking about *getting* right in the dumpster where you're dealing with maggots and spoiled food items. Eventually, I ended up living under a bridge. I took my bath under the bridge in the canal. I didn't worry about the 'gators and all of the different other things that were in those canals. I slept in places a lot of people wouldn't even walk around in, let alone sleep there. I even ate what people left on their tables in the mall, or what they had thrown in the trash.

It was a life of complete insanity.

What was normal to most people became abnormal for me. Working and doing the right thing became abnormal. What became normal was getting high, smoking crack, sneaking in and out of stores shoplifting, then returning to the street and selling the stuff just to get high. It became a vicious cycle, until eventually I'd get caught, and end up in jail. I actually came one point away from being labeled a habitual offender.

The final time I would do jail time, I served a 10 month sentence. This is where God helped me to make a life-changing decision. I looked at my life; I looked at the things I was missing out on with my children, and I looked at this *thing* I had become. So, I made a decision and I said to God, "I just can't do this. I don't want to do this anymore."

Then, a revelation came to me. **Anything God wants to do in our lives, we tend to make complicated, when in fact, all it takes is a simple yes!** So I said to God, "Give me an opportunity to get this thing right, and I will give you 100%." And God said to me, "If you surrender to Me, and allow Me to be Lord of your life, I will give you everything back that you allowed Satan to steal from you." I said, "God, that sounds like a good deal to me!"

I was released from jail on October 24, 2004. It was a Sunday. I left prison with nothing, except a shirt, a pair of pants, and the tennis shoes on my feet. Because I had no place else to go; I finally ended up returning to my Mom's.

As I was sitting there in her living room, my sister came home. She had a young lady with her and they came in briefly to speak to my mom, then left. Now mind you, I had not been out of jail 24 hours yet, and I was sitting there on my mom's sofa when the Lord clearly told me to get up and look out the window.

So, I got up and looked out the window. He said to me, "That's your wife." I said, "Wait a minute! Now I know you're God, and I know you know that I don't have a job. I know you know I just got out of jail." He again said, "That's your wife."

I heard the Lord say, "Because of what I'm going to do in your life, you're going to need someone. If I were to first do this work in your life, you would never take a wife, assuming that she only wants you because of what you have. I'm going to put someone in your life who will walk with you through this process."

So as soon as I could, I asked my sister who her friend was. "Her name is Jackie."

A couple of weeks later, my sister gave me Jackie's number. That was on Sunday, October 24, 2004.

We've now been married 11 years. I have been drug free ever since, and my life has been turned around 180 degrees. Jesus changed my life, and gave me everything the devil stole from me. All I had to do was surrender. I'm now a full-time Pastor who helps many who are hurting to get the freedom that I have received.

Insights with Anh

This is an amazing story where even after being addicted to drugs, homeless, and with no hope, he didn't give up, and God changed his life. Sometimes in our lives, we can feel like we have messed up our lives so much, that our lives aren't worth very much. Failures, the wrongs we have done, and more can plague us where we might feel like God doesn't love us anymore. Some may even be mad at God or wonder if He is even real.

As a former atheist, I questioned God's existence; but looking back, I realize my thought was, "If there was a God, He would never want me". I was a partier who wronged many people. I later realized that God's acceptance is not based on what we do or don't do; it is based on His Love for us. The Bible says "But God demonstrates his own love for us in this: While we were still sinners, Christ died for us" (Romans 5:8). That means The God of the universe who created you loves you just as you are. We don't have to get cleaned up to gain acceptance. He cares so much for you and wants to be in relationship with you.

Finding out God is Real changed my life and was the first step to finding my purpose and the reason I didn't give up. No matter what you have done, it is not too big for Him to forgive. Also, many times people get angry with God because of the circumstances they have been dealt. They say, "Why me God?" But rather than why, a better question would be, "What now God?" We may not know all the answers, but one thing is for sure: God is Not against us. We live in a world where there is evil and people have a free will. Many blame God, but there is another entity on earth who is here to kill, steal, and destroy. There is a verse in the Bible that explains it further in John 10:10.

For those of you who are reading this and you are serious about finding your purpose and fulfilling it, then I'm going to lead you into a prayer that has changed millions of lives. For the skeptic, stay with us as these Real Life stories reveal more truths about God's existence and your purpose.

Prayer: Lord, I come before you in the mighty Name of Jesus your Son. I know I'm a sinner and have done many wrongs. I'm asking You today Lord to please forgive me of all the wrongs I have done. I believe Jesus is Your Son who died on the Cross for my sins. Jesus please come into my heart and fill me with the Holy Spirit. I surrender all of me to You, all of my hopes and dreams, and desires. Wash me Father and cleanse me with the precious blood of Jesus. Please make me whole and teach me your ways. From this day forward I will follow You. Amen

Points to Ponder:

1. How do you feel after saying that prayer?
2. What does Salvation mean to you? What does the dictionary say about Salvation?
3. How will life change today knowing God loves you?

Prayer to Encounter God

This prayer is from Ricardo himself: "In the name of Jesus, Lord God, we give you glory. We give you honor and we give you praise! For anyone who needs to hear a word of encouragement or needs a touch from you, speak clearly to this person. We thank you for what you are going to do. I thank you, Father God for the way you snatched me back and returned everything to me that I had allowed Satan to steal from me. You did it for me and I know you will do it for anyone else who asks you. Amen."

DECEPTION

Evidence that God can Deliver Someone who was Sex Trafficked

What is deceit and where does deceit come from?

Dictionary.com defines it this way: **Deceit** is the quality that prompts intentional concealment or perversion of truth for the purpose of misleading. The quality of guile leads to craftiness in the use of **deceit**: using guile and trickery to attain one's ends.

The Bible also clearly states that deceit takes place when someone believes that a lie is truth.

Wouldn't it be nice if we knew when we were being deceived? Unfortunately, most of us have experienced some type of deception at some point in our lives. I can remember going out on a date with a guy when I was about 17 years old. He was good looking, had money, and seemed like a nice guy. He took me skiing for my first time and later asked if I would go to dinner with him. Why wouldn't I go to dinner with this guy? I agreed and we headed to a very nice restaurant. It didn't occur to me that I needed to keep my guard up at all.

After ordering a Coke to drink, I excused myself to use the restroom. I came back and took one drink and can't remember the rest of the night until I woke up in his apartment. I was fully clothed, but very confused. How did I get here? What is happening? He began trying to take off my clothes and since I was a fighter, I began to fight back. He was confident that I wouldn't escape. I threatened him with whatever threats I could think of. Somehow I fought my way out of his house. It is all still a blur to me. It was so scary not knowing where I was or how I got there. My friend, Matt, figured out a way to locate me, picked me up, and brought me home safely. Apparently, the guy had put "Roofie" in my drink. Roofie is the street name for the drug called Rohypnol. Rohypnol is also called the "date rape" drug. It is illegal in America, but somehow he had it. Though I wasn't a Christian at that time, looking back, I know God was watching over me.

Though she wasn't deceived or tricked by being drugged, Kristina Glackin was deceived by lies, and didn't even realize that she was being deceived. As a consequence, she suffered the ripple effect of believing one lie after another until she found herself a victim of human trafficking.

You will find out how she escaped and despite her situation, she never gave up.

Kristina's Story

I'm going to share my personal pains and trials with you. Although I'm not able to express everything I suffered, my hope is that what I do share with you will help you to overcome your own hardships.

When I was 13 a close family member came to live with us. It was at that time that I learned things I had no idea about. I was still a virgin and not prepared to do what this person was asking. He told me he would give me $500 if I did what he told me to do.

I realize now that I immediately began "acting out" by hanging around some pretty shady friends, smoking marijuana, cutting myself, and suffering from bulimia. I even gave myself away to my boyfriend at the time. All of these coping mechanisms were caused by the extreme amount of internal pain I was suffering. It got to the point where

I took 63 pain pills and cut my wrist in hoping to end it all. I felt myself drifting off and that's when my younger brother came into the room.

My brother knew I had an eating disorder, so he walked to the gas station and bought me a Twix bar (my favorite) and offered it to me. I woke up just enough to tell him, "No thank you," and then he asked, "Well, can I eat it?" Typical brother, right?

When my parents came home from work, they began to give me watered down coke-a-cola—at least, that's what I'm told. All I remember is coming in and out of consciousness and vomiting all over the living room floor. I survived that day by an act of God.

I did return to school with cut marks very evident on my arm which drew attention to me on this particular day. The teacher took me to the counselor's office where I divulged everything I was going through. The counselor immediately took me to my house, put as many of my possessions as he could fit into a plastic shopping bag, and drove me to a group foster home. It was during this time that I began writing poetry, a release from stress that I still practice today, this has proven to be something more powerful than I ever could have imagined.

I continued to do well in school. I loved my foster mom, dad, and siblings. However, after two years in the group home, I was sent to live with who I thought was my biological dad, but soon found out he wasn't. I moved back home to live with my mom and felt safe because that close family member had moved out.

Although I was a straight A student at 16 years old, my brokenness made me drop out of school. I was no longer cutting myself, but I was still bulimic, promiscuous, smoking marijuana, and drinking.

As I continued this vicious cycle, I was seeking the attention of a man that I met in the mall. I told him my story and he was a very empathetic listener. We were friends for a couple of weeks when he suggested that we go to L.A., just a four hour drive, for a concert. He took my I.D. to supposedly create a fake I.D. for me to get into the concert. And, in no time, driving my car, we were off!

However, we never made it to the concert. We ended up at a place where there was a lot of partying going on and where he knew everyone. One of the girl's at the party befriended me and suggested that we take our purses down to my car. She insisted that they would be safer there and to make sure I left my cell phone in my purse. I did, but felt very uneasy about the situation.

Before we made it out of the car to head upstairs, my male "friend" got into the driver side of my car. I was so relieved that we were finally heading to the concert. I sat in the passenger seat while the other girl sat in the back with our purses. Quickly the weight of reality hit me as I noticed this man had a gun in his hand.

He said, "I'll give you all your stuff back, your purse, your phone, your car keys, and your I.D. if you can make me $400 tonight." I immediately knew what he wanted: the same thing that every man I had ever trusted wanted. Staring at the gun in his hand, I swallowed hard, looked him in the eyes and said, "No." He said, "We'll see." He took me to McDonalds, the last meal I would eat for days to come. I ordered a 10-piece nugget meal. By now, they moved me to the back seat of my own car.

They took me to a hotel where I started to feel weird, not just afraid of the situation, but my whole body felt numb and weak. They obviously had put something in my drink. For the following four days, they continued to drug me, threaten me, starve me, and abuse me until I agreed with "the plan."

They took pictures of me and put them on craigslist and sent one man after another into the room. These people sat in MY car, and watched men go in and out of the hotel selling my body for their profit and stealing my dignity. After two days of torture, they left me alone with a different girl. She told me that she had been there for two years and had unsuccessfully tried to get out. She then told me that they planned to kill me if I didn't start to cooperate.

So, what did I have to lose? I mean, this was my seventh day without food. Between starvation and being drugged, I could hardly think straight. When I began to tell each man that was sent to my room about my situation, all I could think to do is ask to use their phone to call my mom. No one would help me; they were afraid of getting in trouble. Finally, after I told one man, he stood up so quick and so straight, I thought he was going to run out the door. Instead, to my surprise, he said, "I'm going to get you out of here!" I was petrified.

After "booking" me for an extended time, he helped me escape down a back staircase and took me to his apartment in Beverly Hills where he fed me Fruit Loops, let me call my mom, and then the police. Unfortunately, the people who trafficked me were never caught, at least to my knowledge.

To make matters worse, when I returned home, I lost my job and home. I tried to pick up the pieces by getting a new job and living with new friends. I was so broken. The bulimia was worse than ever, and so was my drinking habit.

I kept pushing my pain, hurt, anger, and resentment down until there was just nowhere else for it to go. Shortly after, I made the decision to return to my home town. Years later, I went to a psychiatrist for about a month. I told him about my panic attacks and anxiety. He asked about my life, so I told him everything. He diagnosed me with PTSD, OCD, depression, social anxiety, and generalized anxiety. He said it is a wonder I was still functioning at all.

I continued the pattern of trying to find myself in a man. After dating someone for a short time, I got pregnant and became a mom. I had no idea that my child, at three years old, would change my life forever. After putting him to bed one night, I heard what sounded like chanting from his room. When I peeked in, he was sitting up in his bed, staring straight ahead saying over and over "I see God, I feel God,

I see God, I feel God." The next morning, he explained that he was standing with the good God and had to keep saying "I see God, I feel God" until the light came back and the bad god disappeared.

Three weeks later, I was frozen in fear, in the midst of another panic attack. I was so afraid that I had convinced myself that someone was in my house to kill me. I finally broke down and cried out to God. I couldn't take this constant state of fear. My hope wasn't that he would remove my fear, but that He would take my life. I ended in a cry to a God that I didn't know, hoping that He was as real as my son had said.

I soon fell into a peaceful sleep and the next morning, I woke up with overwhelming joy! I had peace for the first time in my life and I just knew that I was loved! Almost immediately my desires began to change. It was like I didn't have to do the same destructive things that I was doing to get through each day. Instead, I already had everything I could hope for in Jesus! I was finally content. He delivered me from alcohol addiction, smoking, and allowed me to walk a celibate life after my second child was born. Yes, I am a single mom, raising two children, but know that it is only through the strength I receive from Jesus Christ that I am living, breathing, joyful, and free of panic attacks. I now use the gift of poetry to glorify Jesus and share my testimony to help combat human trafficking.

While I don't have much in terms of possessions, I have more than I could ever hope for in the Lord Jesus Christ. He knew me and loved me before I was ever created (Psalms 139:13). He knew what was going to happen in my life and had a redemption plan for me whenever I decided to turn to Him. All it takes is humbling ourselves and recognizing that we are NOT God and that we NEED God. He, alone can change our desires, our paths, our hearts, and our purpose. He changes OUR story to HIS story.

Insights with Anh

As a former atheist, I never believed in evil. I used to think morals were dependent on each set of beliefs, and that there was no real right or wrong. Morals were just perceptions, and it was all relative. However, in the light of this story, that belief seems ludicrous. Today, as a Christian, I have found the truth that evil is real and there is a true spiritual entity called the devil.

The Bible states that Satan is the father of all lies and that all deceit comes from him. In fact, in 1 Peter 5:8, this comparison is used: "Your enemy, the devil, prowls around like a roaring lion, looking for someone to devour."

As we see in Kristina's story, Satan often uses other people to be his ambassadors of deceit. Many times, these people don't even realize they are being used and abused by Satan. This is why it is so important to pray for discernment. Often what looks good is actually evil. In 2 Corinthians 11:14 we learn that "Satan, himself, masquerades as an angel of light." How, then, are we to know what is true and what is not?

No other Biblical story exemplifies this as much as the story of the Fall of man in the Garden of Eden. Like the "friend" Kristina met at the mall, Satan disguised himself as a beautiful creature and approached Eve to tempt her. Sadly, Adam was with Eve, seeing the whole encounter, and did nothing to stop it.

The entire account is in Genesis 3, and likely familiar to most, so you may recall that God created a perfect place, the Garden of Eden, for Adam and Eve to live. They were at peace with the animals and their work. Tending the garden was easy. There were no weeds or thistles to hamper their purpose.

God gave them access to anything in the Garden, except told them they could not eat from the tree in the middle of the Garden.

This tree has been referred to as the Tree of the Knowledge of Good and Evil.

Keep in mind that there is always a bit of truth embedded in deceit, or we would discern it right away. And Satan expertly crafted his approach to confuse Eve. He twisted the truth just enough that the subtle lie he included was not obvious.

Satan appealed to Adam and Eve's sense of trust in God's motives. He asked the question, "Did God REALLY say that?" He planted the seed of doubt. Eve played right into his plan by telling him not only were they not to eat the fruit because it would kill them, but they couldn't even touch the tree. God only told them not to eat of the fruit, so Eve herself is embellishing the truth!

Then Satan stated a boldface lie that she believed hook, line, and sinker: "You will not surely die. For God knows that when you eat of it, your eyes will be opened and you will be like God, knowing good and evil." Satan knows how to appeal to our sense of wanting power and desiring to be like God, which is what led to HIS downfall. Ultimately, Satan's goal is to separate us from fellowship with God.

Eve takes the fruit and eats of it, then offers it to Adam, who also eats. The consequences are astronomical. They suddenly realize that they are naked and they become ashamed. They hide from God when he comes to the Garden to walk with them in the early evening, which was their daily routine.

Some theologians believe that before Adam and Eve sinned, their bodies were of a "glorified" nature, meant to live for eternity with God. However, when they disobeyed God and sinned, their bodies immediately began to age and decay. Destined for death, they recognized this gruesome fact and were afraid.

Deceit always has consequences that are revealed afterwards. Some say that "Hindsight is 20/20." If you knew someone was going to break into your house, wouldn't you have been prepared? The Bible

SKELETONS IN THE CLOSET

Evidence God can Help Someone with Severe Guilt and Shame

Do you have a secret that if someone knew about it, you would be devastated? All of us have secrets that we don't feel we can share, even with our best friends.

Before Anh and I were in a relationship, I had done some pretty bad things. Things I had engaged in before becoming a Christian. Things I promised myself I would never tell him, thinking that if he knew he would never marry me.

As we got serious, and eventually engaged, we had some pre-marital counseling. Of course, the counselor insisted that we tell each other about our pasts. Who did we date? What activities were we involved in?

I really pushed back! My attitude was that God forgave me, so no one else needed to know all of that! I had skeletons in my closet that were so deep and dark.

But the counselor pressed me and said that no matter who I married, that person had a right to know my past, my present, and my future dreams.

I can't even begin to describe how torn apart I felt at divulging to Anh the truth about my past. I was sure he would take back the engagement ring and not marry me! But, as I began to reveal to him all of the failures, struggles, and fears involved in my past, something happened that took me by surprise. I felt free! In that moment, I didn't even care if he still wanted to marry me because all of the baggage I had been carrying with me for all of those years vanished and I felt liberated! That actually brought us closer!

Satan stalks around like a roaring lion, tempting us and trying to destroy us (I Peter 5:8). He tempts us on one hand and records with the other. He plans to devastate people. He uses our past sins to try to blackmail us.

But when we confess our sins, we experience freedom and forgiveness! First John 1:9 says that "If we confess our sins, He is faithful and just and will forgive us our sins and purify us from all unrighteousness."

Gina Talmadge is one example of someone who discovered this principle after pledging to never divulge her most sinful secret.

~Kathleen

Gina Talmadge's Story

I was at a vulnerable place in my life where, frankly, I was drinking a lot. I was unhappy with my life, and I had huge anger issues with my friends and family.

Someone close to me was also in a very hard place and going through a divorce. I was under the assumption that the divorce was final, and I ended up having an affair with her soon-to-be ex-husband.

Doctors had always told me that I could never have children, so birth control was never considered. But, I soon began noticing changes in my body. I was 21, and while I suspected I was pregnant, I went into denial.

I lied to myself that I was pregnant for six months! Even though my body was changing, I didn't want to believe it. But I knew in my heart I was. To deal with this, I self-medicated by drinking even more. In fact, I was very suicidal to the point that I walked down the middle of a busy street, hoping that a car would hit and kill me.

Having been raised in the church, I felt shame, guilt, and condemnation because of my affair. And, even though I was totally against abortion, I felt Satan breathing down my neck saying, "Kill that baby. Get rid of that baby any way you can."

I got on the phone to call an abortion clinic. I now thank God it was not an abortion clinic, but a Christian organization! After my conversations with the staff, I was so convicted by the Holy Spirit that I began to weep.

After this, I felt that my only other option was to try to adopt out the baby. I flew to California to an adoption agency where they presented me a book that included couples who were interested in adoption. They suggested that I pick out the parents. So, I did.

Then they sent me for a complete physical. Now, keep in mind, I was still in denial that I was pregnant. I was just numb. When the doctor came in and they did an ultrasound, I could hear the beating of my baby's heart. It was a boy! I began to weep. After seeing him, I told the doctor that I couldn't give up this baby.

Can you imagine how torn I was? I had always been told I could never have a baby, and here I was, seeing the proof that I actually was pregnant! But, I couldn't reconcile was who the baby's father was. In any case, I kept falling more and more in love with this unborn child.

During this time, I was living in the basement at my grandmother's. I stopped eating and isolated myself. I was determined to take my own life. I had known God as a little child, and always saw myself sitting on His lap, so I began crying out to Him. In that moment, that vision of me sitting on Jesus' lap came back to me! I distinctly heard the audible voice of God say to me, "I will be a father to the fatherless. I will help you raise your child, your son." At the time, I didn't even know that this was Scripture from the Bible: Psalms 68:5: "A father to the fatherless, a defender of widows, is God in his holy dwelling."

Hearing God's voice saved my life.

This showed me that God had not left me or forsaken me, even though I felt I had forsaken Him. I knew that He still loved me. As I said, up until this point, I had been drinking so heavily that I was sure this child would be born with deformities or brain damage. After hearing God's voice, I dedicated this child to Him. I was convinced it was time for the secret to come out of the darkness and into the light.

Somehow, without my even coming forth and admitting it, the person I betrayed, sensed that I was pregnant and she came to me, claiming she knew who the father was. This was one of the most difficult encounters we'd ever shared, but in the long-run, it was a huge relief to us both. No longer did I have to keep this secret within myself.

I can't begin to tell you how hard it was to share this news with my family, including the baby's father. It was a long season that included a lot of forgiveness.

Miraculously, while I was pregnant, God provided me with a husband who knew of my pregnancy and knew who the biological father was. He fulfilled God's promise to me of being a "father to the fatherless."

Insights with Anh

More than a story of infidelity or adultery, Gina's is a story of forgiveness.

Some may argue that there are degrees of sin, but in the long-run, sin is sin. Perhaps some sins result in the hurting of more people and some deeper than others, but the same power to forgive the sins of a murderer, is the same power God gives to forgive a person who has stolen gum from a grocery store, or lied about a trivial matter.

Getting Forgiveness: Could God really forgive someone like Gina? Could He forgive an adulterer? In Gina's situation, many people in society might look down upon her and think she committed the worst sin. However, to God, small sins, and big sins, all have the power to send a soul to hell. That is why God saw that we couldn't pay the price for our sins, whether small or big. So He sent His one and only Son as a substitution for us. He would experience the punishment for our sins, while we can experience the feeling of having righteousness. He traded places with us. That is how much he loves you and me, no matter what sin we have committed. When we realize God's forgiveness is available, it is easy to be set free from those sins, whether big or small.

Forgiving One-another: Jesus made a startling statement in Luke 6:37: "...forgive and you will be forgiven." This thought is also expressed in Matthew 6:14: "For if you forgive men when they sin against you, your heavenly Father will also forgive you. But if you do not forgive men their sins, your Father will not forgive your sins." Wow. That seems a bit brutal, right?

Yet, Mark 11:25 underscores the necessity of forgiving others when Jesus said, "And when you stand praying, if you hold anything against anyone, forgive him, so that your Father in heaven may forgive you your sins."

It seems there are conditions for receiving God's forgiveness, which is the willingness to forgive those who have sinned against us.

How is that possible? How can the woman who has been raped forgive the perpetrator? How can the wife whose husband has had an adulterous affair forgive him? How can that mother whose teenaged son was gunned down on the street in a senseless act of violence forgive? And, how can the woman whose sister had an affair with her husband ever forgive?

This is one of the mysteries of God. In man's thinking, it makes no sense; but in God's economy, our obedience opens the door for living in peace and coming to grips with the crazy insanity that seems to surround us. It is a supernatural gift from God. Isaiah 55:8 makes this clear: "For my thoughts are not your thoughts, neither are your ways my ways, declares the Lord."

This is an area where we just have to trust God that asking Him to help us forgive another will, as in Gina's case, help us to be set free of the mental and physical torture from unforgiveness.

The Bible is very clear on how to receive God's forgiveness and the command to forgive others. Not so clear, however, is the importance of forgiving one's self.

Kathleen and I have been witness to the mental, emotional, and physical side-effects of someone not being able to forgive themselves. They become almost paralyzed, focusing so much on their past sins that they cannot enjoy the present, or the hope of the future. I know this was the case for Kathleen for many years of our marriage.

This is a trick of Satan. He wants us to live in the guilt of the past; but Jesus wants us to live in His grace, looking towards a bright future. Once we have received His forgiveness, we are no longer bound to the sins of the past. Of course, we shouldn't be trite about those shortcomings, but in everything give Him praise for the fact that He has forgiven us so that we can live with great hope for the future…both here on earth, and eternity in heaven.

Remember the Word says, "The truth will set you free" (John 8:32).

What is truth? Jesus said, "I am the way, the truth and the life. No one comes to the Father except through me" (John 14:6). Jesus sets us free.

Points to Ponder

1. Have you ever been in a situation where someone has hurt you so deeply that you just didn't think you could ever forgive that person? What was the result?

2. What have you learned about forgiveness from her story?

3. How can forgiveness help you to fulfill your purpose?

Prayer to Encounter God

Heavenly Father, I accept your forgiveness of all of my sins and thank you for the sacrifice you made in shedding your blood, and taking my sins upon yourself. Thank you that I now have eternal life through you because of the free gift of forgiveness you have granted me. Please help me to forgive those who have hurt me and sinned against me; I want to forgive them in the same measure you have forgiven me. And, Father, please help me to forgive myself and live in the grace you give, not the guilt of my past. Amen.

SHATTERED DREAMS

Evidence God Helps when Dreams are Shattered

We all have dreams and "places" we want to go, and expectations as to how those dreams will be fulfilled. There is nothing wrong with dreaming and setting goals. There is a danger, however, if we leave God out of the dream and try go our own way. There is also a danger in our identity of getting so wrapped up in what we DO, that we lose sight of who we really ARE.

Take the model whose dream is fulfilled and she finally is working the runway, only to lose that dream because she gained a few pounds, or a younger face takes her place! Her whole identity of who she was and is has shattered and she doesn't know where to turn. Her dream has become a nightmare, one from which she can't wake up.

She realizes that she's not in control of her destiny after all. And isn't that the lie we buy? We think that if we do all of the right things and set our goals and work really hard, we will achieve our dreams, that we are in control. While these things are good and necessary in the proper proportion, if God isn't allowed to guide our steps, we can easily get off course.

Michael Ray Garvin's dream was to play football in the NFL. But in just a few quick moments, his dream was shattered.

~Kathleen

Michael Ray Garvin's Story

Growing up, all I wanted to do was to play football in the NFL. I attended Florida State and was named All American in both football and track. My whole goal and focus was being good enough to be recruited. In my mind, I was convinced that I could enjoy a 10 to 12-year career in the NFL.

My dream came true the day that the Arizona Cardinals signed me on as a wide receiver and kick-off and punt returner. The first game I played was a pre-season game against the Pittsburgh Steelers where I ran 172 yards, had three 30-yard kick-off returns, and was awarded MVP of the game.

However, two days later, it was discovered that I had torn my meniscus and had to go in for surgery. This was devastating. My dream was shattered. All of these years working toward getting on an NFL team and now this happens?

It was in my heartache and pain that I decided to go back to church. During rehab, I began to regularly attend a church I had visited early in the year. It was a church that one of my teammates encouraged me to attend prior to playing for the Cardinals. Whenever the church doors were open, you would find me there! I attended every Sunday, Wednesday evening, and the Friday night prayer meeting. I recommitted my life to Christ, and even though I was so disappointed that my dream wasn't going the way I had planned, His peace washed over me.

I met my wife there during this time. We were married two months later in that church. It wasn't an easy road for us, but I now know God was preparing us for something big.

In December of 2009, I was signed to the Detroit Lions practice squad, so my wife and I moved to Michigan and began attending Word of Faith Christian Center. I was released by the Lions in April of 2010 and signed to the Las Vegas Locomotives in the United Football League.

I played a full season in the United Football League and after that, ran professional track for the indoor track season. It was during this time that my wife felt God calling her to attend Bible school, so she quit her $51,000 a year job and we moved to Austin, Texas. This was a huge sacrifice for us, but we made it to be obedient to God's will.

I had planned to sign with another team in the United Football League, but that didn't happen. The Lord told me that the enemy - the devil - was going to try to make us regret everything we were doing to serve Him. So, now, my "Plan B" was to use my training certification to train clients and bring in extra income while my wife attended school.

I was working a retail job and trying to build up my clientele for training, but it was not enough for us to make ends meet.

We were not able to make rent, so in February of 2012, we were evicted from our apartment. Finally, after waiting patiently for months, we were able to move into another apartment, but the same day we moved in, my car broke down. I even took on a third job to try to bring in extra income, and it still was not enough. We went through a second eviction in October of 2012.

It just seemed like one thing after another. My wife and kids ended up staying with my mother-in-law while I was sleeping in the gym to help bring in more clients for training. Fifty-five percent of my check went towards supporting my family.

Finally, in 2013, we had a breakthrough. I'm glad that I never gave up. We were able to get into another apartment. It was during this time, in August of 2013, that the Lord revealed to me the ministry He wanted me to carry out called "BelieverZ N da hood."

Though I faced many storms, my faith remained strong. People have asked me if I ever lost hope or faith in God during the hard times, and I say in humbleness, these situations actually brought me closer to God! Staying in His Word and claiming His promises gave me joy and the peace that everything would turn out even better in the long-run.

All you have to do is look at how Jesus and His disciples went through tough times. So, yes, I asked the Lord why we were going through all of this tribulation and He led me to II Corinthians 1:8-10: "We do not want you to be uninformed, brothers and sisters, about the troubles we experienced in the province of Asia. We were under great pressure, far beyond our ability to endure, so that we despaired of life itself. Indeed, we felt we had received the sentence of death. But this happened that we might not rely on ourselves but on God, who raises the dead. He has delivered us from such a deadly peril, and he will deliver us again. On him we have set our hope that he will continue to deliver us."

During this time, God placed a huge burden, and perhaps a *calling*, on my life that I couldn't resist. He led me to go deep into the inner city, 'the hood', to minister to the homeless. I just went out and started preaching the Gospel by myself. Then the Lord told me "there are believers in the hood." And I knew that through the power of the Holy Spirit in these believers, we could share the Gospel together so that lives would be saved and changed. Eventually, one of my brothers in Christ at my church joined me and we set out together to do street ministry.

While I attended Florida State, I would often watch a gangster DVD, which was very influential in a negative way. It was so impressive to me that I wanted to be a gangster. I'm glad I didn't stay on that path. Young kids are very influenced by what they see. As I spent time with the Lord, it was brought to my attention the importance of reaching these young people. God then told me to create a Street DVD.

The videos show true believers preaching Christ, saving souls, and doing good deeds for the people in every neighborhood. I truly believe this street ministry will motivate young kids, youth, and adolescents to grow their relationship with Christ and help lead lost souls to want to be True Believers in Christ!

The Lord wants us to show this generation that being a Believer in Christ is necessary and cool. The youth will see that we dress and look the same, but we're different, we live differently, love deeper, and obey God.

As I look back on my "shattered dream," I totally see how God used just that short time in the NFL to give me a platform from which to reach these gang members and young kids who need the Lord. They will listen to me because of that accomplishment.

Insights with Anh

It is hard for individuals to overcome feelings of depression and hopelessness when their dream in life is shattered. When incidents in life change the course of our lives, it can be devastating. Is there life after shattered dreams?

I tell you the truth, there is Someone who has a dream for you. There is Someone who formed you, fashioned you and even knows every little hair on your head. This is what the Bible tells us. Truthfully, God made you and is totally obsessed with you. And though our dreams can be shattered, His dreams for us cannot. Everything God promises, the devil can do nothing to stop.

"For I know the plans I have for you," declares the Lord, "plans to prosper you and not to harm you, plans to give you hope and a future" (Jeremiah 29:11).

God's plans for us are GOOD plans. His plan includes blessings and a future and a hope. But it is still a mystery unfolding. Sometimes dreams get shattered, but maybe that's because they are OUR dreams, and not God's dreams for us. Many times our dreams for ourselves fall short of God's ability to do far more than we can fathom, think, or dream!

Ephesians 3:20 says that God is "able to do immeasurably more than we ask or imagine." Perhaps God, in His mercy and love, has a way of guiding us to things we can't yet imagine! He reveals them to us as we surrender our lives to Him. That is why shattered dreams are actually possibilities for greater things.

I have experienced this in my life. I had a dream of being a rich doctor, making lots of money, and having a beautiful blonde wife. However, when I came to know Christ, I gave my dreams to Him, and His dream was something I never saw for myself, but it was way bigger than my dream. It was a dream to be awakened, and to awaken the nations with the good news of what God really does in people's lives. Today I own a nationwide business, run a worldwide nonprofit, and that blonde wife, well, I do ministry with her now. God's dreams are always better than our dreams; we just have to put our trust in Him.

Points to Ponder

1. Did you ever have a life-long dream that was shattered?
2. If so, what was your first response? Do you still feel that way?
3. What has been the result of the changed direction in your life?
4. How can a shattered dream bring you to your true purpose?

Prayer to Encounter God

Lord, help us to realize some of the dreams we've had may have been crushed and shattered, but are really just a part of your plan and purpose in our lives. When placed in Your Almighty Hands, our dreams can be reframed and reshaped to fulfill Your dreams for us. Amen.

STOLEN CHILDHOOD

Evidence God brings Emotional Healing even to those who were Molested

Morgan Bryan was sexually molested by her own father from the age of 6 to the age of 12. Sadly, we hear of so many cases of children being abused by an uncle, a brother, a neighbor, a friend, or as in Morgan's case, her own father. It leaves the child confused, hurt, and in many cases, it becomes a life-long struggle that leads to low self-esteem, depression, and even suicide.

When the predator is the father, we can understand how these victims find it difficult, if not impossible, to trust in a God, who wants to be our "Heavenly Father," when abuse has been their only exposure to a parental relationship.

Another common response is for the victim to feel that he or she has done something wrong or that the abuse is a result of something that is their fault.

We can learn much about God's faithfulness and miraculous healing that Morgan Bryan experienced when she cried out to God.

~Kathleen

Morgan Bryan's Story

As a child, I grew up in the Caribbean. From the outside, you would think my parents were model citizens. It appeared they were successful, stellar community volunteers, and great parents. But nothing could have been further from the truth.

My earliest memory of my parents was that they argued constantly. I would try to make them stop, but it only seemed to escalate. Because of the chaos, I harbored fear in my heart and longed for stability.

At age six, my mom and dad divorced. I was heartbroken. Mom moved to Puerto Rico, and for the most part, she stayed away most of my childhood and adolescent years.

Soon after she left the home, the sexual abuse started. My dad and I lived on a farm in the Dominican Republic. To the community, he looked like the hero. The loving dad who stayed behind to take care of his daughter after they were abandoned. No one knew what was really going on when we were at home.

The abuse took place almost every day from the time I was six. He surrounded himself with pornography and sometimes would get me to bring home other children, whom he also abused. I still think of them and pray for them today. It was so confusing, because I was led to believe that this was a normal relationship between a father and daughter. But in my heart, I didn't feel it was right.

By the age of seven, I began to discern that something was not right. I looked at the families of my school mates and realized that their lives were different. So, one day I went to my father and said, "Papi, I have this feeling deep inside of me that I was created for something different. That my purpose is for something different, but I can't explain it."

My father encouraged me to search for that purpose; I thought maybe it could be found in a religion. By age 12, I had tried out at least four different religions. Each one of them left me as empty as before and none of them answered my burning question as to what I was created for and what my purpose was.

I finally came to the conclusion that I was created to be abused. That was my purpose.

My anger continued to grow and my depression was so deep that I lost hope. This is when I started partying and drinking heavily, trying to fill this emptiness with alcohol. It is normal for very young people in the Caribbean to drink and it's legal.

I finally came to the conclusion that I would be better off dead. Why did I need to be alive? I had searched and searched for different religions, I had tried to find this meaning and purpose for my life, but it wasn't working. I wasn't finding anything. So I decided to give up and that I would kill myself.

I started planning how it would happen. First, I tried to starve myself, but that was taking too long and made me very weak. On the outside I would act like I was the happiest person in the room, but when I was alone in my room every night, I would cry myself to sleep.

One night I remember kneeling down in my room and screaming at God. I took a pillow and put it close to my face because my dad was sleeping in the bedroom below mine. I screamed, "Why did you allow this to happen to me? What did I do to you? Why did you even create me?"

I was so mad at Him and told him that all I wanted was to have a family. All I wanted was to have a mom and a dad who loved me. I just cried and cried with every ounce of my body.

At that moment I said, "I don't even think you are real, God. So, in a month, I'm going to kill myself. If you truly came to earth like it says in the Bible, and you healed people who were sick and did all of those miracles, if that was true, then You are going to do something and You are going to reveal yourself to me. Because if you don't, I will kill myself in a month. I will give you a month and if you don't reveal yourself to me in that month, I will kill myself."

I really said those words! I didn't think anybody was listening to me. I had no hope that anyone would respond. So, I started planning my suicide. I decided the best way was to jump off the cliff near my home.

Two days before the month was over, I was lying in bed awake, and all of a sudden my room filled up with this light! A light like I had never seen before. It was a light so bright that I had a hard time even keeping my eyes open. I remember feeling this overwhelming peace throughout my whole body. At that moment, there was no fear; there was no doubt that the Person who was visiting me that night was God. God, the Father.

I tried to speak, but the peace was so overwhelming it was difficult to get a word out! As I opened my eyes I could see rays of light that were all different colors. Colors that I had never seen before. I wanted to stay in that Presence so badly. I didn't want to go back to my life of pain, shame, and depression.

At this point, I pleaded with God to "just please take me with you." Out of the light, I heard this voice. It was strong like thunder and at the same time it was a peaceful voice. As He spoke, it came into my body, into my mind, and I felt even more peace. Peace overflowed in me by just hearing this voice.

Again, I said, "Please take me with you!" But, He said, "No, it's not your time yet. I will use your testimony to heal many people." I had no idea what he meant by the words he said, but the one thing I did know is that I had hope again. It was so powerful to hear his voice and have this experience with him. Then the Light just faded away.

My depression was gone instantly! My sadness was gone instantly! And there was peace in my heart. The next day I remember feeling this heaviness lifted off my shoulders. I still had not given my heart to the Lord, but this encounter changed my life.

For a time, nothing in my circumstances changed, but then one day I received a call from my mom telling me that she had a terminal illness. She asked if I would come and take care of her.

I had experienced this encounter with God that was incredible and gave me hope, but there were still things in me the Lord needed to do. I decided to go and take care of her.

A neighbor invited me to a small church. I wasn't even curious as to what religion it was. I just said, "Okay, I'll go with you."

When I got to the church, there was no sign on the outside telling me what kind of church it was. They were teaching about the lost sheep and how the Lord left the 99 sheep to go get the one lost sheep. They asked if anyone wanted prayer, so I went to the altar, kneeled down, and cried. No one at the church knew me or what I had gone through. But, this preacher came up to me and the Lord started showing him everything I had gone through.

I heard the Lord say, "All of those nights that you cried yourself to sleep, and asked where I was, I was right there with you."

I began attending this church and found out that it was a Christian church that believed in the Lord, so I started seeking the Lord and received Jesus in my heart. One day I told the Lord that I felt there was something He wanted me to do. He spoke to my heart and said, "You need to go to your dad and ask for forgiveness."

This sounded crazy! Why should it be ME that needs to ask for forgiveness? He was the one that hurt me. But, I told the Lord I would obey Him and do this.

I went to my dad and said, "Papi, if I ever did anything to hurt you, please forgive me." He cried like I'd never seen him cry. With tears pouring down his cheeks, he said, "No. I'm the one that has to ask for forgiveness." Through this, the Lord restored my relationship with my dad so incredibly that I was not fearful of him anymore.

Thanks to the power of forgiveness and my obedience to the Lord, we were restored to the point where my dad walked me down the aisle when I got married.

The Lord also restored my relationship with my mom, but it was very different from how He restored my relationship with my dad. I went to her and said, "You left and hurt me and I felt abandoned, but I want you to know that I love you." This wasn't easy. I had to ask the Lord to put a love in my heart for her. And the Lord did put a love in my heart for her. One day, I confronted her with love. "Mom, I want you to know that what you did to me really hurt me, but I do forgive you and I love you."

She froze. She didn't have any words to say and she couldn't believe that I was telling her that. As a result, the Lord has also restored my relationship with my mom. She even has a great relationship with my two amazing children. The Lord gave me a husband and restored my relationship of sexual intimacy with him and has totally healed me.

Insights with Anh

Sexual abuse usually leaves the victims scarred for life. According to the National Center for Victims of Crime, 1 in 5 girls and 1 in 20 boys is a victim of child sexual abuse. And these are only the ones that report the crimes. How many more have become victims, yet don't tell anyone? Yet, the consequences can be severe for victims of sexual abuse, ranging from post-traumatic stress disorder, depression, and the abuse can even lead to hyper-sexuality. There are a myriad of effects caused by sexual abuse, and the effects are difficult for psychologists to treat, because the abuse literally changes the way the brain interprets and responds to the world. How can one get healing? I have met countless women who have been healed from their abusive pasts through a relationship with Jesus Christ. Jesus said that He would make all things new. How wonderful that is for someone plagued with horrible memories of the past!

Morgan received healing to such an extent that she was even able to extend forgiveness to her father. Could you do that? I know that Morgan was only able to do this by the power coming from her faith in Jesus Christ. Forgiveness in extreme situations like this seem inappropriate, but in truth, forgiveness is what set Morgan free.

Forgiveness is not always a "once and for all" kind of thing. For many, it is a continual activity. Kathleen and I have heard of a woman who also suffered terrible abuse by her father, and like Morgan, desperately sought to forgive. She discovered that it was a process. At first, her hurt and unforgiveness would surface almost a dozen times a day. But each time, she would pray to God, "Please help me to forgive." In a few weeks, she discovered that the past abuse was only coming to her mind a few times a day. And, finally, she realized that she seldom thought of it at all. Forgiveness freed her of that bondage!

If you, or someone you know, is or has been in an abusive situation, they need to know they are not alone and not without resources. We know there are so many victims who feel threatened and may not tell anyone about their abuse for years, if at all. But, we want their voices to be heard and for them to know that there is healing power in trusting in the Lord, Jesus Christ. We pray that you have the courage to accept the love others have for you who want to help.

Points to Ponder

1. Has anyone ever done something to you that hurt so much that you determined you could never forgive them? How did that affect you?
2. How do you explain Morgan's motivation and ability to forgive her parents?
3. What happens when you ask for forgiveness and the person doesn't accept that apology?
4. How can forgiving or being forgiven help you to fulfill your purpose?

Prayer to Encounter God

Father, we thank you that you've brought redemption and healing through the act of forgiveness. There may be someone reading this who has also lost hope and is so angry. Lord, please reveal Yourself to this person, as You did to Morgan. Let their heart be open to Your love and the reality of Who You are. Please restore this person, first from the inside, and allow that to flow to the outside. In the name of Jesus, Father we pray that you bring the restoration power of forgiveness into our lives.

NEW AGE & CONFUSED

Evidence that God reaches those who lose their mind and feel Hopeless

Other than talking about the weather, probably one of the most common pick-up lines is, "So, what's your sign?" Astrologers claim that by studying the stars, sun, and moon, they can successfully predict someone's future, or future events. However, many embrace this as a true science. Astronomy, NOT astrology, is a true science where the stars are studied from a factual perspective.

Some studies reveal that close to 70% of predictions made through Tarot cards and astrological signs fail the test of being fulfilled. It is another way that Satan draws our attention away from truth.

Another commonly held belief is that UFOs and Aliens are real. Steven Bancarz was so caught up in this that he threw his Christian heritage away to pursue the study of the mystics.

Steven's Story

I am a former New Age blogger who used to have a website called *Spirit Science and Metaphysics*. This site was up and running for about two years, collecting over 100 million website views. I was also a lead author on another well-known website. This website covered a wide range of New Age beliefs, which I genuinely believed to be correct at the time.

Things like Pyramid Technology, Pantheism, the Unified Field of Consciousness, the pineal gland, astral projection, and ancient astronaut theory were put on the site. I would formulate my research in such a way that left no option but to be agreed with.

I didn't always believe this stuff. I was actually born and raised in a Christian home, but when high school came around, that went out the window pretty quick—especially when I started researching the topics of UFOs, aliens, and alien abductions. This opened up a new world of information to me which convinced me there was something more to the world than the Biblical worldview that I was taught.

I backed up my research with primary studies, peer-reviewed alternative journal articles, and proper referencing to attempt to justify a New Age worldview that contained some of the following beliefs:

That we are all God and everything in the universe is made up of God. That the soul lives on in a neutral spirit world before reincarnating; that psychic ability is safe and real, and that past lives give us insight into our personality, character, and life situation.

I also believed that astrology is real, meditation is essential, and that Jesus was an ascended master of some kind who taught a universal path of enlightenment, but was not God-incarnate (God with us).

I believed that ancient aliens visited us in the past and gave us technology, culture, and wisdom; that pyramids held special energetic properties that made them healing machines; and that it was safe to consciously induce an out-of-body experience. The list goes on and on. This is the trail I traveled for about five years.

During this time, I was also in school studying to be a philosophy major at the University of Guelph in Canada. I fully believed in my heart that Christianity was naive and ignorant of the ultimate nature of reality. I thought I had it figured out, or that I at least had the basic principles figured out, which gave me a solid foundation to work with. But one problem remained.

There was something about Jesus I couldn't put my finger on that kept knocking at the back door of my conscience. I always had to try to explain Jesus away; account for what he said, and construct a worldview that accommodated him and his ministry in some way. He was just too powerful, too influential, and too special to simply write off.

This intuitive spiritual attraction towards Jesus never really left me. In fact, prior to and during my turning to New Age beliefs, I was obsessed with the work of William Lane Craig, a Christian apologist with a ministry named *Reasonable Faith*. I didn't buy into the Christian doctrine, but I loved the arguments for God and the philosophical training.

In 2012, I created a Facebook page dedicated to sharing alternative information I had come across. In January of 2014, I launched the website, *spiritscienceandmetaphysics.com* and began my life as a full-time New Age blogger, making a living off teaching what I now know is false doctrine.

In fact, for a while my site was the largest New Age site *in the world*. This was largely due to the fact that I had a lot of social media connections to other pages.

The website was a "success" by worldly standards. The first month I made over $50,000 from advertising revenue alone. Apparently, this is what over 130,000 website views a day on an ad-optimized site will get you. As a 21-year-old, I was excited, of course. More than excited, I was cocky, arrogant, greedy, vain, egotistical, selfish, and narcissistic to extents you would not believe.

Despite my deep moral flaws, I still believed I was doing the right thing. I believed my success was being *caused* by the universe agreeing with what I was doing. This is taught in the New Age movement—that the universe is a guide and a caregiver. I used to pray and thank *the universe* for giving me a chance to help enlighten people and wake them up into higher consciousness.

On the outside, I was living the dream. I was working from home, was my own boss, and the money provided me the car and house I wanted. I felt I was blessed in a lot of areas of life and that my career as a New Age teacher (of sorts) would continue to develop.

I was 100% convinced of reincarnation and of esoteric material. I even had several "out of body experiences" confirming to me that what I was researching was effective and bringing me closer to uncovering the truth about the nature of reality.

But even with all of my success, I felt terribly unfulfilled. Something was off, messed up, and seriously missing from my life.

This emptiness led me to try to fill the void in my life with, well, sin. I was lustful, greedy, a liar, and a cheater. Looking back at myself, these words are understatements for how truly broken I was.

What I now know was sin, began to catch up with me. I had to face reality. I had to come to terms with the life I was living, and more importantly the people I had hurt. Up to this time, I had isolated myself in many ways, which led to the false belief that I was in control of my life and it was up to me to fix myself. However, I soon learned that I didn't have the ability to fix myself. Broken can't fix broken.

It slowly dawned on me that I was depraved. I thought I knew it all, but I was also a slave to sin. I was confident in my worldview, but it wasn't bearing any good fruit in me. It was as if I had become infected by a disease that kept growing deeper and deeper into my being.

It was at this point when I knew I had to stop suppressing my spiritual intuitions about Jesus and give Him a chance. Out of desperation and an intense need to be repaired, I finally sought Him. I needed to be brought out of the delusions and sin that had ruined my life.

It was a few weeks after I made that decision that I fell on my face before Him on my back balcony, weeping and reaching out to

Him. I was just so sorry and so broken. I don't want to under-emphasize how broken I was. My life was in ruins, along with my psychology and emotions.

My soul was destroyed. I had tried doing life my way, but had hurt myself and many people along my path. I just wanted the truth and I wanted Him in his fullness. For the first time in my life, I totally gave myself to Him.

When finally, in sincere surrender, I did this, the spiritual atmosphere started to change around me. His personal presence actually filled the atmosphere; everything around me seemed overcome by his Glory. There was a personal, divine, authoritative presence all around me. I knew He was Lord over me and everything in creation!

I KNEW IT WAS JESUS. NOT NEW AGE JESUS, BUT THE JESUS OF THE NEW TESTAMENT. THE JESUS OF SCRIPTURE. THE JESUS I GREW UP SINGING ABOUT IN SUNDAY SCHOOL. THE JESUS WHO I SUPPRESSED IN UNRIGHTEOUSNESS. IT WAS **JESUS CHRIST**.

My spirit and mind was coming into alignment with the discovery of who He is. And let me just say this: When we come into His presence, all doubts fade away. It's done. You know the truth when it's right in front of you. You know He is Lord of everything. You know everything in creation is under His feet. You know He is sovereign.

You know He loves you and is perfect in all His ways with a holy, righteous, and glorious radiance that is out of this world. But for me, what struck me most was that I knew exactly where I stood in relation to Jesus, and where Jesus stood in relation to the world.

He was King; I was a sinner. The universe is subject to Him. I just knew that is how it is. I was overwhelmed with this feeling that He was God over me and everything around me. He stood over everything in creation, and in that moment, everything in creation seemed to honor Him. Somehow, in the spirit, I detected that the wind through the leaves and the sounds of the crickets seemed to point to Him and glorify Him—as if they were somehow acknowledging and even praising Him!

This is the reason I say I encountered Him—because I did! It may sound strange, weird, or unbelievable, but this is the best way I can describe what happened. I was confronted with the Lord. He revealed Himself to me, and He has lived inside my spirit ever since. He has not left me since that day.

Light bulbs were going off like crazy as the Holy Spirit started to show me the truth about the New Age topics I was involved in. The scales fell off my eyes to reveal the carefully crafted approach of occultism under the guise of a universal love. I began to see the same patterns and traditions repeating themselves in every culture EXCEPT the people of Scripture.

Suddenly, I saw that the New Age movement sought to orient everything away from Jesus by baiting us with a false, self-serving theology. Everything was carefully set up to keep us from Jesus Christ.

The reality of this was revealed to me in such a startling way that I quit my job the next day, sold my house and car, and moved back in with my parents. Immediately, I started going to an amazing church, got baptized, and began the sanctification process of a lifetime. I stopped searching for the truth because God had revealed it to me. And for the first time in my life I began growing in the truth.

The Lord put in my heart the desire to create a new website. He wanted me to reveal the things I had learned from my past to help make the Christian faith as rational and intelligible as possible to the unbeliever. I wanted to provide reasons for faith in Jesus and expose false worldviews that distort the truth about who He is.

Jesus is real. He loves you, died for your sins, and wants to spend eternity with you. And we can know Jesus is real on a personal level because His Spirit enters into ours when we believe on Him and are saved. It's not about being "churchy," or just trying to be a better person; it's about direct fellowship with the Holy Spirit of Jesus. This personal relationship is available to anyone who will surrender themselves and call upon the name of the Lord.

Insights with Anh

Wow! There is so much to Steven's testimony. Volumes of books have been written trying to explain the mystical elements that led him into an intellectual quest for knowledge and truth. For a time, he was convinced that the New Age Movement satisfied him.

With that said, I do want to give a biblical perspective on a few of the commonly held New Age beliefs. Keep in mind that false doctrine always has many elements of truth intertwined in its philosophy. But, most ideas are twisted in such a way that we are led AWAY from, not TO Jesus Christ.

For instance, Steven mentioned that one of the tenants of New Age thinking is that "we are all God, everything in the universe is made up of God. The soul lives on in a neutral spirit world before reincarnating and that psychic ability and phenomenon is safe and real."

This is a derivative from what Christians essentially believe, but is a far-reaching idea that pivots away from what Christ teaches in the Bible. New Age is about discovering that you ARE God, and that everything around you IS God. However, this is the same sin that Satan committed. He wanted to "be like God" and therefore was cast down out of heaven. Many times in the Bible it is clear that God will share His throne with no one, because truly, no one is qualified to take that position. However, the idea of everything being one with God, and being God, is transgressing that line of God being God, and people being people.

However, Christians believe that when they accept Jesus as their Lord and Savior, they are given the gift of the Holy Spirit. "The indwelling of the Holy Spirit is the action by which God takes up permanent residence in the body of a believer in Jesus Christ. Jesus revealed to His disciples the new role the Spirit of Truth would play in their lives: "He lives with you and will be in you" (John 14:17). The apostle Paul wrote, "Do you not know that your body is a temple of the Holy Spirit, who is in you, whom you have from God, and that you are not your own? For you are bought with a price; therefore glorify God in your body" (1 Corinthians 6:19–20).

These verses are telling us that the believer in Jesus Christ has the third Person of the Trinity, the Holy Spirit, living in him. God being in us, yes, but us being God, that is very far-fetched. When an individual accepts Christ as personal Savior, the Holy Spirit gives the believer the life of God, eternal life, which is really His very nature (Titus 3:5; 2 Peter 1:4), and the Holy Spirit comes to live within him spiritually. The fact that the believer's body is likened to a temple where the Holy Spirit lives helps us understand what the indwelling of the Holy Spirit is all about.

The New Age theory would deduce, then, that everything and everyone has God's Spirit, and is God, but the Bible makes it very clear, that those who call upon the name of Jesus will receive the blessed Holy Spirit.

Another thing Steven was fascinated with was the idea of Aliens and UFOs. I did quite a bit of research on this, and must say that I was surprised to discover that many theologians DO believe in Aliens and UFOs! In fact, many gave succinct biblical references and teachings to support their findings.

However, their conclusions may astound you as to the origin of these foreign bodies.

To understand this, we must first remember that we are made of body and spirit. Our fleshly bodies are of a natural origin; our spirits are of a supernatural origin.

When Satan and one-third of the fallen angels were cast out of the 3rd heaven, they were still spirit beings that could take on different natural identities. The first biblical instance of this is Satan disguising himself as a beautiful serpent in the Garden of Eden to deceive Adam and Eve.

There are many biblical accounts of fallen angels, also known as demons, taking on different appearances in the Old Testament. Some, like the Nephilim, actually inter-married with human women who gave birth to giants. Goliath was one of these.

So, back to Aliens. It is a commonly held belief among Bible scholars that Aliens are demons taking on the physical likeness of a being that we mistakenly assume is from another planet. This even explains the mysterious lights, "flying saucers," and instances of unidentified aircrafts that elude modern-day radar. See the end of the book for links to do further studies on this subject.

Points to Ponder

1. Before reading Steven's story, what were your assumptions about New Age beliefs? Have they changed in any way after this study? If so, how?

2. What are your thoughts about Aliens and UFOs? Do you think they could be demonic?

3. What do you think was at the core of Steven's decision to forsake the New Age beliefs and recommit his life to Jesus Christ?

4. How can the Truth bring you freedom and purpose for your life?

Prayer to Encounter God

Lord teach us truth. Help us to discern false doctrines and untruths. Please work in our lives to deliver us from any deceptions that may be working in our lives, and bring us the glorious truth! Lies bind us; let your truth set us free. We receive the Holy Spirit, the Spirit of truth that will guide us all of our days. In Jesus' name, Amen.

SEXUALLY ASSAULTED

Evidence that God can heal those who have been Sexually Assaulted

In the United States alone, over 290,000 people are sexually assaulted each year. And these are just the statistics documented from people who came forward and reported the attack. Many suffer in silence and blame themselves for someone else's offense.

These feelings are prevalent any time we feel violated. My sister's home was broken into and ransacked and all of her valuables were stolen. Not only did she feel violated, but this incident made her feel unsafe.

People who are victimized often suffer the blame, the pain, and the shame, when in fact, they did nothing wrong. It just demonstrates how Satan can so warp the truth that the innocent one feels guilty!

Jenn's story demonstrates how through the trauma of being victimized, God provided a way for her to have healing and the ability to help others.

~Kathleen

Jenn's Story

I was raised in the church by Christian parents and would by all accounts be labeled as "normal," or "above average." I married a godly man and things were going along really well. However, after we had been married for 10 years, I was raped by someone whom I had only known for a few weeks, and was well-known in our community.

Before I went to the hospital, I remember walking into my house and being enveloped with a cloud of shame, feeling that it was all my fault. I laid down in my bed and just remember thinking, "I'm going to go to hell now." I felt like now I wasn't good enough to walk out whatever call God might have on my life.

During this time, my husband was incredible. He was loving and encouraged me; we even drew closer as a result. But there were some stark realities we had to face. Because I didn't go to the hospital right away for the rape kit, the medical staff warned me that there was a possibility I could be pregnant. There was also the fear of a sexually transmitted disease. How would we handle these things?

We both immediately agreed that if I were pregnant, we would have the baby. However, we were unclear as to whether we would be able to keep that child, or give it up for adoption. As it turned out, I was not pregnant and once the results of the rape kit were available, there was an investigation. It was discovered that this person had not only done this to me, but over many years, had raped others as well. However, I'm the only one who followed through with an investigation.

But, even though we were drawing closer, both my husband and I were very angry and were harboring deep feelings of unforgiveness towards this man.

A couple of weeks after the rape, my husband was asked to speak at a men's retreat out of town and ended up staying with friends of ours. His anger towards this person had so escalated that he was absorbed to the point of not being able to focus on anything else.

During the night, he had a dream, and in the dream, he walked up to a mirror and looked into it. Rather than seeing HIS reflection, what was looking back at him was a grotesque image that was so ugly and repulsive he had to look away. When he woke up, he asked the

Lord what the dream meant. God told him that without Him and His forgiveness, this is who he really is. And that the same forgiveness God portioned out to us on the cross is the same forgiveness that he expects us to impart to those who have violated and defiled us. This dream has and will forever impact us both, and as a result, for many years, we prayed together for this man.

Throughout my life, even from being a young child, I was a worship dancer at my church. That was how I expressed my love to God. After this experience, however, I didn't feel worthy to be in His presence. I didn't feel I was good enough. I felt dirty. I felt shame. I didn't feel beautiful anymore. For at least two years after the incident, the shame factor weighed heavily on me. There were many times during the two years that I was asked to join the dance worship team, but I just couldn't do it. However, one day I decided to give it a try again, so I went to rehearsal.

Anyone who has ever been a dance worshipper knows that it requires total abandonment. Once we started the dance and I was in total worship to God, I started to cry for the first time in two years. I went backstage, curled up in the fetal position behind a Ficus tree and sobbed for over an hour.

It was during this experience that a dear friend comforted me and reminded me that forgiveness is a powerful thing, and unforgiveness paralyzes and destroys a person. It was at this moment, being so rock bottom, that I had no place else to turn but to God.

The Bible tells us that Jesus is the healer of our heart. He is the One who forgives without condition. He is the One who wants to take that burden from us. He is the One who took all of our sin and shame with Him and nailed it to His cross.

So, I cried out to Him and said, "God I'm done with this. I want to be free." I knew the only way I could be free was to forgive the person who did this to me. Lying behind that tree in the fetal position, I was able to forgive. I can't even describe the peace and excitement that washed over me! I've learned that forgiveness is a process. Sometimes I have to visualize this person and forgive him on a daily basis. Through God's healing power, I truly am set free! I'm so glad that I didn't give up.

Insights with Anh

Jenn's story is one of healing and restoration. When we think of healing, we usually first think about a sickness, disease, or physical wound that needs treatment and as a result will heal. Christ came, however, to not only heal our physical illnesses, but "all our infirmities." An infirmity is defined as a physical or mental weakness.

In Isaiah 53:4, we read that "Surely he took up our infirmities and carried our sorrows." It is clear that God wants to heal us not just physically, but emotionally as well. This verse also clearly reveals that we WILL have sorrow, that we WILL suffer emotional setbacks, but that He has provided a way for us to overcome our pain and to have joy!

So, how do we go about receiving this healing? Let's face it. We can't just pick up the phone or Google a website that can make us an appointment to receive freedom from the emotions that bind us! We can't buy this on Amazon, charge it on our debit card, and expect it to be delivered in the mail in a few days! But, as we see in Jenn's case, when she was willing to cry out to Jesus and tell Him she was ready for His supernatural attention, she was immediately released from the emotional pain and shame that had defined and shadowed her life for two years.

The Bible contains numerous stories about how Jesus, as the Great Physician, healed those who asked Him. Although many of the accounts are of the physical healings, which was outwardly apparent, we know that in each situation, there was also a spiritual healing that freed the person emotionally.

One such story is that of the paralyzed man whose friends had the gall to interrupt Jesus' preaching and break through the roof of the hut where he was teaching. They dropped the man on his mat right in front of Jesus (Mark 2: 1-12). What love these friends had for this man, and what faith they had in Jesus!

I'm sure they just assumed that Jesus would understand that they were asking him to make their friend walk and were expecting that He would reach out, touch him, and heal him. Nope. Jesus says something that seems very disconnected from a physical healing. He says to the paralytic, "Your sins are forgiven." What???

While there are many lessons to be learned in this encounter, one which demonstrates that He and only He can forgive sins, Jesus is painting a picture of His understanding of the importance of healing the ENTIRE person: body, spirit, and mind. The paralytic was healed only after he was in right relation with Jesus.

Points to Ponder

1. Have you ever been in a situation, or known someone in a situation, where you or they felt violated or betrayed? Explain.
2. How did you (they) react to the perpetrator?
3. Do you wish that you or they could have reacted differently? If so, how?
4. What advice would you give to others who have experienced emotional pain and mental torment because of situations that made them feel violated?

Prayer to Encounter God

Jesus, You, alone, are the Great Physician who can forgive our sins and heal us from the inside out. I pray for Your healing touch on those reading this who have been violated and suffering from the after-effects with shame, blame, and pain. Please give them freedom through your healing power and help them to be in right relation with you. Amen.

ANGRY AND ABUSIVE

Evidence that God can set Alcoholics Free

Have you ever said, "I will never be like my mom, or my dad?"

I once heard it said that the very thing we fear, we draw near. Sometimes we draw near it unwittingly, or unknowingly, but little by little, we inch our way in that direction.

I know that in my family, I have seen history repeat itself. A family member said they would never be like another family member, but sadly, ended up being just like him. And Anh also experienced this with his father who was a very anxious person. Anh was determined not to be like that, but as he came into adulthood, he too suffered extreme anxiety.

One of the most powerful truths about our relationship with God, the Father, is that no matter how our earthly fathers may have failed us, when we come into God's family, we are "re-fathered!"

What pathway can we follow that will lead us into breaking the cycle of influences that are harmful, and adopting attitudes and behavior that lead us to a new beginning?

Perhaps Jared Calhoun's story will provide some valuable insights for us.

~Kathleen

Jared Calhoun's Story

From the time I was five years old, until my father abandoned the family at age 16, getting beaten up by my father was almost a daily routine. And the reason? There was none. My father was just plain angry, violent, and had little respect for anyone.

A beating would go on until he just got worn out. It was usually for nothing, and it often went on for long periods of time. I developed an anger towards God because I knew my father was coming home and I would ask God, please don't let this happen to me. But it still happened.

I felt as if my pleas fell on deaf ears because the abuse continued.

Some people get into a difficult situation and then ask God to help get them out of it. I never was willing to do that. I just expressed to God my anger at allowing the abuse to happen, but never asked how to get out of it. As a result, I resolved to take the situation into my own hands. I decided that if God wasn't going to be there for me, I would just deal with it on my own.

Even though the abuse ceased at age 16, the next three years continued to be tumultuous for me.

By age 19, I experienced what would some say was an epiphany. I realized that I had turned out exactly like my father. I was very violent, abusive, and disrespectful towards women. And I was very angry.

This gripped and scared me to the point that it motivated me to begin attending AA meetings. But something happened there that continued to anger me. They actually told me I needed to turn to a Higher Power. What? I needed God in my life? That was a problem, without God. So far, I hadn't done such a great job of solving my problems on my own, right?

After not talking to anyone for almost two years, what would my voice sound like? I cleared my throat and hoped that what came out wouldn't be too scratchy. With trepidation, I reached my sweaty hand out to touch the door handle.

I froze. I remember staring down at my shoes and for the first time noticed the threadbare laces. I took in another deep breath, dropped my hand, and hurried away.

For the next two weeks, you could find me wandering the area as I had become used to, begging for money, lifting my thumb to hitchhike, and just trying to escape my misery. Strangely, several who consistently gave me rides encouraged me to consider Teen Challenge.

Finally gathering my courage, I approached the building again. This time, with only a little hesitation, I reached for the door handle. The weight of the door was heavy. It dawned on me how lean and weak I had become. I cautiously entered the welcome area.

Smiles and open arms greeted me. I soon discovered that Teen Challenge was a Christian, adult drug and alcohol deliverance program. Of course, my first thought was that it hadn't gone so well for me at AA, but I was so desperate, what did I have to lose? And did they have food, a shower, and someplace to sleep?

They did.

Here, God spoke to me through the Bible. It was here that I finally listened.

During one Bible reading of John 12:32, I felt God was speaking directly to me: "But I, when I am lifted up from earth, will draw all men to myself." Then, in that sweet, almost audible voice God uses, I felt him saying to me, "I know that you have gone through a lot of hard stuff, but I came to this earth and was crucified on the cross for you. I went through something even worse than what you have gone through and I went through it personally FOR you to SAVE you."

I was instantly reconciled with Him! I couldn't believe that He would actually come to this earth and do what he did on the cross for me. I gave my heart and life to him and I just had this peace come over me…such peace about my life that I started feeling joy again. I started having happiness again. I had hope in my heart again. As I read the Bible more, I realized that he wanted to use my life. He wanted to take all of these things that had happened to me, turn them around and use them for His good.

The process of being delivered from drugs and alcohol was not an easy journey. In fact, it was long and arduous. Dealing with the addiction was one thing, but even tougher for me was dealing with my angry emotions. Where had this anger come from? How different would my life be if I could somehow contain it?

Helping me deal with my out-of-control emotions is one of the greatest things that Teen Challenge taught me. I learned that through prayer and through leaning on Jesus to help me with certain things in my life, I became freed from this bondage.

If I were to show you a picture of me before Teen Challenge next to a picture of me today, you would swear that it was not the same person. And, well, I'm not! Being re-fathered changed me inside and out!

I am currently enrolled in Teen Challenge Bible College in Los Angeles and I want to serve the Lord with all of my heart.

Insights with Anh

I, too, was determined not to walk in my own father's footsteps. My father struggled with bipolar disorder, anxiety, and depression, and it caused a lot of problems in our family as I was growing up. My family told me it was genetic, and so I lived my life thinking that I was susceptible to those things. So I did whatever I could to not fall into the footsteps of my father's ailments and behaviors. However, as I grew into my teens, I found myself struggling with the same issues my father did; I began to have anxiety all throughout the night where I couldn't sleep. Plagued with fears of failure, and fears of my destiny, I didn't know what to do. However, the cycle of anxiety was broken when I found Jesus Christ and accepted Him as my Lord and Savior. It was a night/day experience.

Setting an example and being a role model are powerful responsibilities. And, as was in Jared's case, many people who vow they will never hurt someone as much as they were hurt, routinely fall back into this pattern of behavior.

Often, the daughter of an alcoholic will marry an alcoholic. Victims of abuse sometimes continue the cycle of abuse and hurt their own children the way they were hurt.

The Bible is quite clear about abuse patterns, and depicts these things as sin. Sin has a way of following family patterns and spreading. In Romans 5:12, it says "Therefore, just as sin entered the world through one man, and death through sin...death came to all men because all sinned." The Bible is alluding to the fact that sin patterns can be spread from one person to another, and that sin originally started with the first persons infected, referring to Adam and Eve.

You can see this laid out in the story of King David, who was one of the most notorious kings in the Bible. His sin of adultery with a woman named Bathsheba, and then murdering her husband, Uriah, to hide the adultery, was a gruesome act, and could be called a horrendous sin. But you can see that sin spreading into his blood line when afterwards his son, Amnon, raped his own daughter, Tamar. Through deception, he lures his half-sister, Tamar, to bed with him and rapes her. Here we see the perpetuation of the cycle of abuse and sexual immorality. Then, as David committed a murder, his son Absalom commits murder by murdering his brother Amnon to avenge his sister's shame. The Bible paints a clear picture that sin moves and spreads from person to person, even down one's bloodline from generation to generation.

So, where is God in all of this? Perhaps like Jared, Bathsheba, or Tamar, you have been, or know of someone, who has been a victim of domestic violence.

In Biblical times, there were no social service agencies, no church programs, or school resources for victims to turn to. But today, there are many resources that people can turn to for help.

The most helpful resource that I have found is the Lord. When we humbly turn to God and ask him to help us, He will help us, no matter the situation. He comforts us and meets our needs. In fact, once Jared asked for a relationship with God the Father, he realized that even though his earthly father had failed him miserably, he was miraculously re-fathered through his relationship with Jesus Christ.

All of us have had family members, co-workers, and friends fail us, but if we cry out to Jesus, He will open our eyes to the plentiful substitutes He has assigned to help fill the void of need in our lives.

David cried out to God and repented of the terrible things he had done to Bathsheba and Uriah. God heard that prayer and blessed them with another son. His name was Solomon, and it is said that he was the wisest man who ever lived. He went on to build a great temple and lead his people to strength and prosperity. Solomon was able to break the cycle of abuse because he turned to God and asked Him for wisdom. Christ has the power to break family patterns of sin, as we call out to Him to change us. Only He can make old things new. And when someone is made new, the sins of the past no longer cling to them. In II Corinthians 5:17 it says, "Therefore if anyone is in Christ, he is a new creation; old things have passed away; behold, all things have become new."

Points to Ponder

1. Has there ever been a time in your life when you felt that God turned His back on you?
2. If so, did you turn away from God, or try to draw closer to Him?
3. How would you counsel someone who has been a victim of domestic violence?
4. How can calling out to God in our own mess help us to fulfill our purpose?

Prayer to Encounter God

Heavenly Father, thank you for letting us be re-fathered and for being the parent and friend who never fails us. Jesus, thank you that you are my personal way to the Father, and that I can find new life, breaking away from patterns of sin in the past. Thank you for being there when I humble myself and cry out for help. Thank you that You are my source and all I need. I know that people might let me down, but when they do, I can turn to You. I love and praise You!

LIFE AFTER ABORTION

Evidence God can Forgive and Heal Those who have had an Abortion

What is the correct answer: Pro Life or Pro Choice? In today's culture, this is a controversial topic. Whose rights are more important: that of the unborn child, or the woman having the right to make decisions about her own body?

I do believe that many women make the choice to have an abortion out of fear. What will others think because she had an affair that resulted in a pregnancy? Many are young girls who fear what their parents will say, as well as their peers. Some are pressured by their boyfriends to get an abortion. We even know a married couple with two children who considered aborting their third, thinking they couldn't afford another child. But through a visit to a pro-life clinic, they decided to have the baby: a beautiful, healthy baby boy!

Early on, some of my friends decided to have abortions because they thought that was their only option. They were young and believed having a child would ruin their career, education, and ultimately their future. I can remember asking myself what I would do if I got pregnant? One of my friends, who I later talked with about it, said she regretted her decision to have an abortion. Another lady I interviewed said the abortion procedure injured her internal organs so that later when she tried to have children, she wasn't able to.

My husband and I were invited to speak together at a church service one Saturday evening and at the end of the message it was pressed upon my heart that there were women in the audience who felt so much shame and regret from having an abortion. They believed that God could never forgive them for what they did. As I began to pray and announce that abortion is not the ultimate sin and that God can forgive you, women began to come up for prayer. Their hearts were broken and tears filled the altar. Though they regretted their decision, they no longer felt condemned by God. It was a wonderful night of breakthrough and healing.

Our story is with Joyce Zounis Brown. Joyce didn't have just one abortion; she had seven. You will see from her experience that having an abortion isn't as simple as some would have you believe.

~Kathleen

Joyce's Story

My first abortion took place when I was 15, and my seventh when I was 26. I remember walking through the doors of the abortion facility with my mother and she looked at me and said, "We will never talk of this again."

Never once during the seven abortions was I told that I was carrying a child, but rather was referred to as "a blob of tissue". I was never told how my life would be forever altered and the trauma I would suffer, including the need to grieve and cry for my unborn babies.

It was 1977 and at age 15, I had no intention of being a mom. I took my babysitting money, made the appointment, and had the abortion. When I left the clinic, they claimed that I should just give it 20 minutes and my life would go back to normal. The truth is, your life NEVER goes back to normal after having an abortion.

Abortion affects you mentally, physically, emotionally, and spiritually. There are several stages of grief that follow an abortion—and one is denial. Studies show that from about five to 20 years after an abortion, a woman does everything possible to suppress her abortion memory. Alcoholism, drugs, and even suicide are common after-effects.

Many begin to think they're going crazy and that they are the ONLY one who is feeling the desperately painful emotions of anger, depression, betrayal, and confusion. The reality is, most who have walked through that clinic door, exit it to suffer in silence.

One would think that after experiencing this devastating choice, you would never go down that road again. However, in the next 11 years, I had six more abortions. Though I knew the Lord, the only way I can explain it is that I had my agenda, and was determined to be in control of those plans. If something didn't fit into my plan, I took action. A baby did not fit in with my goals and aspirations.

As I look back, I would have to admit that my motivation was fear, as it is with many women who make this choice. I feared I wasn't ready; I feared I couldn't afford to have a child on my own; I feared what my friends would think of me; I feared being alone.

I know now, however, who the author of fear is, and that is our enemy, Satan. God is the creator of life. Satan is the destroyer of life. In God there is forgiveness; in Satan, condemnation. Only those honest with God can receive pardon from sin.

I eventually married and was pregnant with my second living child. I must give credit to my then three-year-old son for giving us that wake-up call that totally changed the direction of our lives. As most children do, they mimic what we say, and one day I saw him putting his fingers up to his mouth and inhaling, copying my husband and me smoking pot. That shocked us both to the point that we decided it was time to go to church.

So, wouldn't you know that on our first visit to a church, the pastor spoke on abortion! I felt as if there was a neon light shining down from above my head flashing, "Murderer! Murderer!" But, God began the healing process right then and there. It began with me acknowledging to myself what I had done, and not again running away from the truth because of fear.

Soon I found my way to a pregnancy care center, something I never even knew existed during those 11 years. I picked up a pamphlet and began to read. It was like someone had followed me with a camera for 10 years and had captured exactly, the after-effects of abortion, which I learned is called post-abortion syndrome.

This pregnancy care center offered a Bible study for women who agonize from the loss of their children through abortion. The study not only walks women through their pain, but the healing that is possible through the forgiveness of Jesus Christ. While in this Bible study group, I will never forget when I understood that abortion is a sin; a sin that IS forgivable.

With honesty and undone silence, thirteen years after my first abortion, pride, pain, and struggle surrendered as I told the Lord about my shameful sorrows. The agony in all that I had selfishly sacrificed, from our relationship to publicly mourning my children, was restored. His redemption not only rescues us from ourselves, but breathes new life and hope. God takes the ugliest of sins and restores beauty from the ashes.

The enemy – the devil -- would like a post-abortive woman to believe that her sin is so bad she can never be forgiven. That is a total lie! There is freedom and no condemnation in Jesus Christ (Romans 8:1). We can also take hope from Psalms 103:12: "As far as the east is from the west, so far has he removed our transgressions from us."

I would never suggest to a woman to have an abortion. It is not only physically painful, but emotionally, mentally, and spiritually. If I could do things differently, I would. My hope is that other women would consider their options and realize abortion isn't a simple procedure; it is a life-long procedure of healing from this decision. I thank God for bringing healing into my heart and for forgiving me for the choices I've made.

Insights with Anh

Joyce's story is not a story of condemnation! It is a story of healing and forgiveness. It is one that she desires every woman who has ever chosen abortion will embrace as a way to be set free from the pain and guilt of post-abortion stress syndrome. Before we talk about how to receive healing and forgiveness, let's look at what Post Abortion Syndrome means. Post Abortion Stress Syndrome (PASS) is the name that has been given to the psychological after-effects of abortion based on Post Traumatic Stress Disorder (PTSD). It is important to note that this is not a term that has yet been accepted by the American Psychiatric Association or the American Psychological Association.

Nevertheless, any event that causes trauma can result in PTSD, and abortion is no exception. No matter what your background is— philosophical, religious, or political views on abortion -- we have found that having an abortion can affect women not only on a personal level, but can potentially have psychological concerns. The process of making an abortion choice, experiencing the procedure, and living with the grief, pain, and regret is very difficult for the majority of women we have interviewed.

Many women will try to hide their emotions and don't understand why they feel the way they do. All too often there are women who begin to not only hate their choice, but hate themselves as time goes on. They might keep track of the day they made the decision to abort their child and as the years go by they say "my child would've been this age." "I wonder if he would've looked like me?" Uncontrolled thoughts will surface and it's like pouring salt in a wound. Those who experience guilt wonder, "Could God ever forgive me? How could I even forgive myself? Will I have to live with this hurt and condemnation the rest of my life? Is there help for me, or is this just the consequence I need to live with?"

If you are reading this and you or someone you know has had an abortion or maybe even multiple abortions, I have good news for you. Jesus not only can forgive you, He desires to forgive you and can heal your soul.

Someone once asked me, "How could Jesus forgive me after I had an abortion; didn't I commit murder according to the Bible?" She was referencing one of the Ten Commandments, which says, "You shall not murder." Many people look at the Ten Commandments as a set of rules that, if followed, will guarantee entrance into heaven and a good relationship with God. However, the purpose of these laws is to prove that no one can perfectly obey them. One might wonder, "why would God make laws that no one can obey?" That's a great question, but as you get to know the Word of God, it is clear that through the law, we realize our great need of God's mercy and grace.

We have all broken at least one of the Ten Commandments. In God's eyes, there is no pendulum on doing wrong or committing sin. Sin is sin, whether it is a sin of lying, cheating, stealing, coveting, giving false witness, committing adultery, dishonoring our parents, etc. If any of these things are done by us, then we have fallen short of God's expectations.

The good news is that we don't have to live in shame, guilt, torment, and fear of God's judgment. Though He doesn't condone our wrongs or sins, and even though we may face consequences for the choices we have made, He doesn't want us to be separated from Him.

The Bible tells us in Romans 2:4 that "the goodness of God leads you to repentance." It's His Love that brings us to Him. He desires to have a relationship with each of us regardless of who we are or what we have done. As Joyce discovered, we can boldly go to the throne of grace (Hebrews 4:16) to "find grace to help us in our time of need." When we turn to Jesus and admit our wrongs, ask for forgiveness, and receive it, He is faithful to forgive and bring us back to a restored relationship with Him.

Post-abortive women have often asked Kathleen and me what has happened to that unborn child. We believe that child is with the Lord! We also believe this is the case with women who have miscarried and those who have lost young children. Though there is no solid Biblical reference to this, Kathleen had a situation that happened to her that she doesn't share with many people. On the delivery table while her mom was giving birth to her, Kathleen died twice. She can remember floating up in the air and seeing the room. As a little girl she would tell her mom about the hospital room where she was born. Her mom was always shocked, but believed it was possible, as doctors didn't think Kathleen would survive after her heart stopped beating twice.

We have heard of people who have died and come back to life. Some of them have shared how they saw miscarried babies reunited with their moms in Heaven. One man said, "I saw babies who were miscarried and aborted grow up right before their mother's eyes."

Points to Ponder

1. Have you ever committed what you consider to be the "unpardonable" sin, whether an abortion, adultery, or bringing false witness against someone that led to their demise?

2. After hearing Joyce's story and considering God's Promises and Possibilities, what is your perspective on that now?

3. How would you now respond to someone who is considering an abortion?

Prayer to Encounter God

Father, God, thank You that when we confess our sins, you will forgive them. Thank you that when we repent, you remove our sins as far as the east is from the west! I pray for those who are hurting to turn to You as you are the healer of our souls. Amen

WITCHCRAFT'S DECEPTION

Evidence that God can bring someone out of Witchcraft and Darkness

When I was growing up, I considered myself to be a very spiritual person, and I started doing some things that I thought were okay. I assumed that anything spiritual was good. For instance, when my grandma died, we tried to call her back from the dead. As only 3rd and 4th graders, we said things like, "Grandma, if you can hear us, move this doll."

It frightened us when creepy things actually started to happen in that room. The doll's head started moving and it was really scary! Needless to say, we ran out of the room screaming! I believe it is possible for us to open doors to spiritual things that can prove harmful as well as good. For instance, God has often intervened to comfort and direct his followers through dreams; however, Satan can also use dreams to frighten and misguide us.

Especially today, people seem to assume that anything spiritual is a good thing and the thought that evil might be involved is nothing but hocus pocus. However, the Bible makes it very clear that there IS a spiritual realm and in that realm, there is a battle going on between good and evil. There's light and there's darkness. One will cause good; the other, evil.

~Kathleen

Maura Cruz Lanz

Sadly, like so many who live in darkness, my childhood was full of verbal and physical abuse. At one point, my father divulged to me that for a time when he was growing up, he had lived with his grandma, my great grandmother, and that she had been a medium. She was very renowned to the point that people would line up at her front door as early as 5:30 a.m. to be in the front of the line to see her and hear her predictions.

When my mother was pregnant with me, she traveled from Cuba to the United States to have my great grandmother lay hands on her belly to "pray for me," and at that time, she predicted that I was going to carry on with her power. So, the thought of having spiritual powers was no new idea to me.

At age 13, one of my friends brought over a Ouija Board. There were several of us in the room, and to our amazement when no one was touching the planchette, it started moving all by itself! It was a bit scary, to say the least! But from this experience I slowly opened the door to having my Tarot cards and horoscope read, and allowed myself to experiment in this spiritual realm.

We were really poor when I was growing up. In fact, we lived in the Projects where my dad worked as a server and my mom, a seamstress. But somehow, my parents budgeted enough money to enroll me in a Christian Day School from age three to age six. My parents didn't go to church, but during this time in my life, I was exposed to Bible stories and at age five, I asked Jesus into my heart. I didn't really understand it all at the time, but one thing was certain: I knew that I loved Jesus! I would often just say, "Oh, Lord!" He was my everything. The best time of my life was during those early years.

After age six, my parents enrolled me in a public school. This led to my being molested by a teenager, and from there, my life spiraled out of control. I began to suffer a lot of insecurities and fears. During this time, I also began seeing scary things in the dark, a pathway likely opened up through my great-grandmother. I believe that fear is a tool the enemy uses to get a foothold in a child's life.

The Occult, however, was already in my blood line. It is a curse I believe I was born with. However, God in His sovereignty, allowed me to attend that Christian Day School so that I could hear the truth about Jesus; to know Who He is and What He can do.

I felt very misunderstood by my family and didn't understand why I was treated the way I was. Can you believe that I was married at age 15? By the time I was 17, I had given birth to a son, but the marriage was unbearable. My husband would severely beat me and then leave me alone, abandoned, for weeks at a time.

I was eight months pregnant with our second child when he wrapped an extension cord around my neck and began to hang me. I literally saw my life flash before my eyes. All I could say was, "Jesus. Jesus. Jesus." On the third time, my husband let go of the cord, fell to his knees, and ran out of the place like he'd seen a ghost. Shortly after, at age 18, I left him and filed for divorce.

My mom insisted I go with her and visit a Santeria, a woman known to be a High Priestess in a cult, which is prevalent in Cuba. Their motivation was to prepare me to go through the rituals to become a Santeria. She later admitted that the reason she took me there was because I looked so lost and had no direction. Everyone was hoping this would give me purpose and provide a degree of happiness that I desperately lacked.

They put me through the entire training process. But just before they could finalize it, something happened that kept them from finishing it. I truly believe it was God's hand of protection on my life, honoring my simple childhood acceptance of Him.

Even though I never became a Santeria, I allowed myself to get deeper into the New Age movement, which led to charting horoscopes and doing readings. I would sit with a brandy sifter filled with water in front of me and look in it. I could see things! I would see the spirit guides and I would see other people's spirit guides. I know now that these "spirit guides" are demons manifesting themselves as a familiar spirit.

They would actually speak to me and even though they were rather transparent, I could see them. In fact, they would actually transform themselves into a human-like form. They took on different forms and appearances such as an Arab or a gypsy.

Eventually I met and married the man who is currently my husband, and during this time, I got deeper and deeper into Santeria. One of the beliefs in this demonic occult is that they require making sacrifices. These are made to certain demonic gods that they believe have the power to protect them, give them prosperity in their jobs, and lead them to love and marriage. They were putting their hope in their spirit guides.

I allowed these demons to take over my body to the point where I could feel them entering me and then allowed them to use my voice. They would speak through me and use my body to perform their actions. The irony is, I found myself without prosperity and falling deeper and deeper into a dark depression; just the opposite of what the occult said I should be experiencing!

My husband and I were fighting all the time and had seriously discussed divorcing. This was such a dark time in my life that I would have visions of driving my car full-speed into a telephone pole to commit suicide. The temptation was almost overwhelming.

I don't think anyone around me at the time realized how unhappy and desperate I felt. Working at a radio station as an account executive, pastors from our area would come to the radio station to record their programs. One day I was filling in for the receptionist and one of the pastors who came in happened to be a childhood friend of mine. He took one look at me and said, "Maura, can I pray for you?"

I flippantly said, "Sure, you can pray all you want." And I'm thinking to myself, "Oh, my goodness, what a Jesus freak!" And I started making fun of him in my head! This was on a Friday where I routinely left work and went directly to where I allowed myself to go into a trance and practice witchcraft. This night was no exception.

The following Friday when this same pastor came into the radio station to record his show, I began to see things in a different light. I started doubting what I was doing. You see, I actually thought what I was doing was for Jesus! I truly thought that I was working for God. This led me to praying one simple prayer. I said, "Jesus, if what I'm involved in is of You, show me. If not, I want to know Your truth."

Shortly after that prayer I attended my nephew's first birthday party. My sister lived just two doors down from me. We all walked over to her house where the whole family was gathered for the party, including aunts, uncles, and cousins. In our Cuban culture, we all routinely say, "If God willing," or "Lord willing." We always acknowledged God, but we didn't have a relationship with Him.

At the party, I found out that my sister and uncle had started reading the Bible. I admitted to them that I could read anything out of the Bible, New or Old Testament, but I could never read the Book of Revelation. And how odd that was. My uncle looked me dead in the eye and said, "That's because you are with the devil."

I was shocked! How could he say that when I would give the shirt off my back to help anyone!

He said, "You cannot be with God and the devil at the same time." Oh, boy, did that make me angry. I stomped out of my sister's house and walked down to my place where I knelt at the altar that was in my house. I actually had a Bible sitting there. I thought I believed in God and that I was doing God's work and God's will.

I grabbed the Bible and went to my front room where I sat down on the couch. I opened up the Bible to the Book of Revelation. Suddenly, the wall behind me started resonating as if at least 10 people were pounding their fists against it. I was home alone. This frightened me to the point that I slammed the Bible shut. But do you know that all of a sudden, a blanket of peace filled that room and the noise stopped instantly!

At that moment, I was so filled with a hunger to read the Book of Revelation that I opened up the Bible and began reading it.

The most amazing thing happened; I wasn't just reading it, I was SEEING it, like watching a movie! I read it in its entirely in one sitting and when I got to the end, the last word was "Amen." Out loud, I said, "Amen," and when I did, something flew off my eyes. I looked up at the ceiling and around the room, it was if I was seeing it for the first time. And it was MY house! I felt like a sack of weights had been lifted off my shoulders. I turned around to look, but didn't see anything. But I felt it. Then in the pit of my stomach I knew that Satan had used me and deceived me all my life.

I balled up my fist and I held it against my mouth and said, "I renounce you, Satan, and all your works." I said this three times and on the third time, I clearly saw iron bracelets with chains attached to them open up and fall off my wrists.

By now, I was freaked out! Then the vision disappeared and I heard a voice that was like rushing water and thunder at the same time. The voice said, "Now you're going to work for ME! The same things you did for Satan, you will now do for Me." It was literally like he took the old me out, and replaced it with the new me. Instantly I was flooded with joy, with peace, and with love. His love is so amazing!

That night I decided to destroy that altar, but then heard a still, small voice say, "No! Wait!"

The first thing I did the next morning was to call the pastor, my childhood friend, who prayed with me, and told him what had happened. He started screaming, "Hallelujah! Praise God!" He and his wife rushed over with their newborn son and he prayed with me. Together we destroyed everything on the altar. He anointed my house and prayed over it. I had lived so long in darkness, but now, light flooded my life and my soul!

Insights with Anh

I always thought that witchcraft and religion were just fairytales and hocus pocus. However, with my eyes being opened, I realized both have an element of reality to them; they are real forces, yet opposing one another. In my Christian walk, I have encountered people who were demon-possessed, just as described in the Bible, where they would shriek and fling the person around violently. The amazing thing is that no matter which country I encountered these demon-possessed people, they all responded to the name of Jesus! There was one common root to all those whom I interviewed afterwards—all had been connected in some way or the other to witchcraft.

There are several instances in the Bible where God makes it clear that we are not to meddle in witchcraft. One of the more detailed accounts involves King Saul, who ignored God's instruction, and visited a medium/psychic that the Bible calls the Witch of Endor. You can read the account in I Samuel 28:4-25.

King Saul violated a decree that he himself instituted, based on instructions from God recorded in Deuteronomy 18, that specifically prohibit the consulting with Familiar Spirits, or mediums. In the story, Saul has so disobeyed God, that he cannot get answers from God through the avenues God originally ordained, including dreams, prophets, and the priests.

So, Saul, who totally ignored the prophetic advice from the Prophet Samuel when he was alive, was so desperate for instructions that he violated his own law (based on God's) and sought a medium/psychic, believing this person could actually tell him how to proceed in the war encroaching upon the Israelites. However, when he opened the door to darkness, his disobedience in not listening to God brought about tragedy.

When we need answers to life's questions—the best way to do so is to seek God. The greater truth we learn through this story is that when we obey God, just as in Maura's case, He is faithful and more than willing to provide us divine insight and instruction that guides us.

Points to Ponder

1. Have you ever visited or thought of visiting a medium/psychic, or someone who says they can predict the future through your horoscope or tarot cards? If so, what was your motivation? How did it turn out?

2. How did Maura's story impact your thinking about witchcraft and familiar spirits?

3. Could spiritual doors that were open and are not from God keep you from fulfilling your purpose?

Prayer to Encounter God

I want to end this chapter and pray again the prayer that Maura recited: "I renounce you, Satan, and all of your works. I renounce you, Satan, and all of your works. I renounce you, Satan and all of your works, in the Mighty Name of Jesus!" Lord, God, just as with Maura, break those chains that have bound us to Satan's power and release us into your loving arms. As I am renouncing Satan, Lord Jesus, I am receiving You into my life. Cleanse me spiritually from the inside out, and make me clean by your blood. I receive it, and will walk in it forevermore in Jesus' name. Amen.

LIFE AFTER DEATH

Evidence God is Real -- Life After Death

According to Kerry Foy, who 'unexpectedly' experienced Heaven - Heaven IS real! Many of us have heard stories of people who have supposedly died and then come back to tell about their experience. But there is always that lingering doubt that what happened to them is not real. Or is it?

When I worked in the hospital as a Chaplain-in-training, I met with several people who said they experienced something supernatural when they died. It's fascinating to me that they all said they saw a light and then heard, "It is not your time, go back". Many people have these experiences, but fear that no one will believe them, so they keep it to themselves.

Dying and coming back has a name: NDE, or near death experience, but these are people who HAVE actually died, so what was near death in these experiences? In fact, in most of these cases, the doctors pronounced as dead, the person who miraculously came back to life. Where were they during that time? Do their stories agree?

Is there an afterlife? Or do we just dissipate and become nothing?

~Kathleen

Kerry Foy's Story

I was a single dad, and I believed in God, but I pretty much just lived in the world. In fact, you would consider that I was just living a rather average life. I was raising three kids on my own and just trying to get by.

I was caught up in the ways of the world, struggling with the stresses that life brings. Without a connection with Jesus Christ, my anxiety was just compounded. However, this all changed in a split second.

In 2005, I moved to Colorado with my three kids to live near the woman who is now my wife. We had only been there for three weeks when my life-changing event took place. She and I had just dropped off her three sons for the weekly visitation with their father. He didn't appear to be home.

Up to this time, I had never met her ex-husband. I had only heard stories of his abusive behavior in their 13-year marriage.

We were about to leave when a vehicle pulled up and blocked us in the driveway. The Ex jumped out of his car, very angry and confrontational. He ran over to my side of the car and barreled in on top of me, pinning my arms. Strapped in the seatbelt, I was defenseless. He beat me relentlessly, throwing punches to my face and head. He then tried to strangle me into unconsciousness.

I could feel my life slipping away as he was strangling me. I couldn't breathe and knew I only had a few more minutes to live. I screamed out, "God, please help me!" Then everything went black and silent.

Immediately I was transported to an indescribably wonderful place. Suddenly everything was so bright! And the sounds I heard were of the most incredible music and singing. I found myself in a beautiful, amazing garden. It was so overwhelming and indescribable that I began crying! Then, Jesus Himself appeared before me. He was so blindingly bright and warm. He held my hands, knelt with me, and prayed. He spoke to me in a language I had never heard before, but I understood every word he was saying. His touch to my hands and then my face was so overpowering, amazing, and healing.

He was telling me that everything would be okay and that I would be okay. I remember Him saying, "You're safe now, but I'm going to send you back because you still have work to do."

While in heaven, I had the overwhelming feeling of warmth and peace. And as I said, I heard the most angelic and amazingly wonderful music and singing. The garden we were in was indescribable in its beauty. Jesus and I were kneeling together and He was holding my hand. I couldn't really see His face, but His whole countenance was very bright.

Up to this incident in my life, I would describe myself as someone who believed in Jesus, but was not "in" Him, not serving Him. However, as the beating progressed, I cried out to God to make it stop. This led me to truly be IN Him and desire to serve Him. He is faithful when we cry out to Him!

When it was all over, between eye-witness accounts, the doctor's assessments, and the extent of my injuries, it is estimated that he threw between 250 and 300 punches to my face and head, resulting in 14 major facial fractures and too many minor fractures to count. In fact, even my eye socket was fractured and I was left with severe brain trauma.

I'm not sure how much time elapsed during my experience, but the eye-witnesses say it was at least 20 minutes. For me, it seemed like much longer. As I was coming in and out of consciousness, all I could think about was my three children and what would happen to them if I didn't make it through this.

The next thing I know, I'm back in the vehicle and the ex-husband is no longer in the vehicle pounding me. I felt as if I was struggling to stay alive at this point, but took heart in the words Jesus had spoken to me.

In spite of all the injuries, it has taken much more time to heal emotionally and mentally than to heal from my physical injuries. My physical healing was miraculous; I actually didn't even need any surgeries! I truly believe that was a result of the touch of Jesus that I experienced.

It was more challenging to overcome the emotional/mental post-traumatic stress disorder (PTSD) that this incident initiated. For me, the turning point came when I finally, truly, turned my life over to Jesus Christ and got saved. I sincerely gave my life to Christ at this time, which I had not done before. You see, you can BELIEVE in God, but until you RECEIVE Him, you do not have a relationship with Him, or the power He gives us through His Holy Spirit.

From this point on, I never suffered from PTSD again.

Before this incident, I used to have a terrible temper. But, now I am calm, have patience, and have confidence in my life after death.

Jesus is real and not just a theory! Heaven is real! Trust me that surrendering our lives to Him and asking Him to forgive our sins and give us eternal life is the only way we will experience peace in this life and live with Him for eternity in the afterlife.

Insights with Anh

When I was an atheist, and especially as a scientist, I really did not believe in heaven or hell. I reasoned that it was because science could not 'prove' it. If science can't prove it, then it doesn't exist. Or at least that's what I thought. But since then, I have experienced many things that science has not been able to explain. I now know that heaven is VERY real! I've come to understand that through the power of Jesus Christ we can actually bring heaven into our situation.

The Bible teaches that as followers of Christ, to be absent from the body means to be present with the Lord (2 Corinthians 5:8). Countless people share their stories of dying, and having experiences of seeing Jesus and the similar things that Kerry saw. Science disregards this as a chemical reaction in the brain before someone dies. But how can that be, when even brain-dead people have these types of encounters when dying? Sometimes, even people from other faiths besides Christianity see Jesus in their near-death experiences, as well. There is so much evidence, but many doctors ignore the possibility of God being real. These experiences point to the reality of God and Jesus.

Why do people fear death? It could be because it is something that they have never experienced before. They question what it will be like…really cool or a bit boring with just a bunch of people and angels singing for millions of years?

I asked my pastor about this one time and he told me the story of a woman who died and came back to life who described her experience. She talked about being able to see colors that don't exist on earth and being able to breathe under water! We know what the Bible teaches: in heaven, there will be no tears and no pain. Jesus called it, "Paradise".

The streets in the Kingdom of Heaven are made of pure gold. Just think… the dirt under our feet in heaven is gold! We are also told in Revelation 22 about the River of Life. It is as "clear as crystal, flowing from the throne of God and of the Lamb, down the Great Street of the City. On each side of the river stands the tree of life, bearing twelve crops of fruit, yielding fruit every month.... There will be no more night...for the LORD God will give them light." To some this may sound like a fairytale, but as I do more and more research, I am finding out that this place exists. Many who have died and come back alive describe their experience to match much of what the Bible alludes to. It would be catastrophic to ignore the reality of there being such a place.

Jesus proclaimed in John 14: 2-3, "In my Father's house are many rooms (some translations say mansions); if it were not so, I would have told you. I am going there to prepare a place for you. And if I go and prepare a place for you, I will come back and take you to be with me that you may also be where I am."

What I have found is that we should NOT fear death! In fact, we should be excited that death allows us to be with our heavenly Father. We will actually hear His voice in that mysterious language Kerry referred to and will know Him for all eternity! Through Jesus we will actually experience paradise! Do you realize that you have access to this realm here and today? Jesus said, "I am the way, the truth, and the life, no one comes to the Father except through me" (John 14:6). If you receive this Jesus, you will find The Way. As a Molecular Cellular Developmental Biologist, I have discovered this truth. It has totally changed my life. Forever.

Points to Ponder

1. Do you believe in an afterlife? Why or why not?
2. Have you ever known someone who has experienced an "NDE," or near death experience? If so, what was their story and conclusion?
3. Do you fear dying? If so, why? If not, why?
4. How could knowledge of the afterlife change your purpose?

Prayer to Encounter God

Father, God, I lift up our readers who identify with or are intrigued with Kerry's story. I pray that you would bring healing to all who might be suffering from situations similar to Kerry's, who seek physical and emotional wholeness. May your Kingdom come and Your will be done for total wholeness for those who have suffered from PTSD resulting from traumatic situations. We thank You that you are real and that we will see You on the other side. Jesus, we want to receive you now, so we can know the reality of heaven living through us today. We believe and receive you now. We repent of our sins, and follow you. We give You all the glory in Jesus' name, Amen.

HELP WITH ANXIETY & DEPRESSION

We must learn the Truth that will set us Free. Jesus came to bring us life and life more abundantly. He doesn't want us to live our life in fear, regret, anger, self-hate, and depression. The Bible says "the devil is here to kill, steal, and destroy" (John 10:10). If you feel like your life is a mess and God hates you, let me bring you hope.

God doesn't hate you! He loves you and wants to see you set free, so you can live out your purpose here on earth. You are created in the image of God. The enemy – the devil hates you. We are in a battle daily. The Bible says, "We wrestle not against flesh and blood, but against principalities, against powers, against the rulers of darkness of this world, against spiritual wickedness in high places" (Ephesians 6:12). If you struggle with self – hate or depression, there are a few things you can do today to help you to gain freedom and peace. Kathleen and I have written down a short list below.

1. God Loves you – (John 3:16). For God So Loved the world that he gave His one and only Son whoever believes in Him will not perish, but will have eternal life. Ask God to help you to understand just how much He loves you. The world may come against you, but when you know God is with you and that He loves you, it won't matter if anyone is in your corner, even during your hardest struggles. Also, the Bible says God demonstrates His own Love toward us in that while we were sinners, Christ died for us (Romans 5:8). That means you don't

need to work your way to His Love. He will take you as you are and He will heal you from your heartache and pain.

2. You're Not Alone – Knowing that you are not alone and others do understand where you are coming from is so helpful. Kathleen used to feel like no one understood her and that they would think she was crazy if they knew the bad things she was thinking or feeling. When she shared her thoughts with me, I would say "yeah, I've had that thought… but I don't need to dwell on it or take it in as my own." It brought her much relief knowing that she wasn't alone and neither are you. Also, the Bible says God will Never Leave you or forsake you (Hebrews 13:5).

3. You Are Not Crazy! God has not given you a spirit of fear, but Power of love and a sound mind (2 Timothy 1:7). Realize the thoughts you are having are not necessarily yours. You might think something, but there is an outside voice trying to plant seeds in your mind. Isn't that a good thought knowing that those evil or odd thoughts are not your own? You have the power to fight off wrong thinking. Another good thought is knowing that your brain can only think one thing at a time. You have self-control, which means you can choose what you think even if it seems you have no control.

4. Emotions - Do not allow your emotions to be your guide; instead, let your actions be your guide and your emotions will follow. Go against what you feel and do the opposite. Example: I don't feel like getting up, but I'm getting up and I will push myself to do something new. Maybe take a short walk, feel the wind outside, listen to the birds, breathe in and out and take pleasure in the little things.

5. Thankfulness - Start thanking God for the things you do have even if you don't feel like it. Write a list of things you are thankful for. Example: Thank You God that I can see, smell, hear, taste, etc. When we complain and grumble, life will get

harder and harder. Thankfulness is a huge key to healing. 1 Thessalonians 5:18 says to give thanks in all things.

6. Start Singing - Sing worship music – go on YouTube and search for worship songs and start praising the Lord. The Bible says God inhabits the praises of His people (Psalm 22:3).

7. Be Love - If you don't feel loved then Go Be Love! Yes, love is an action. 1 Corinthians 14:1 says to "pursue Love". Plant seeds of love. What you desire to receive, give to others. Example: Go give someone a hug, smile at someone, do something kind for someone. The Bible says you will reap what you sow (Galatians 6:7). Start sowing love and you *will* receive it back.

8. DON'T LOOK BACK! - You cannot change what you have already done. God's mercies are new every morning (Lamentations 3:22-23). Regret keeps you from the present and future. God did not give us eyes in the back of our heads for a reason. Forgive yourself and move on.

9. Forgive Others - As Jesus hung on the cross he said, "Father forgive them for they know not what they do" (Luke 23:24). Can you imagine forgiving someone as they are spitting in your face, beating you up, and finally taking your very life? Jesus did just that. As we forgive those who hurt us, we begin to be free ourselves from the bondage that has held us. Forgive as you have been forgiven – (Matthew 6:14).

10. Repentance - Repentance is not just feeling bad about something; it is turning away from it. If you struggle with a certain thing and you know it's wrong, but can't seem to stop, say, "Jesus, please help me with this. I no longer want this in my life. Please take this desire away from me. Forgive me of my sins." As you release that thing and continue to seek the Lord, He will bring you freedom. Start to hate the things that are hurting you or others.

11. You are One of a Kind! – Did you know there never was or ever will be another you? The Bible says you are fearfully and wonderfully made – (Psalm 139). Just take a look at your finger print and you will see that no two finger prints in the entire world are the same. God has a plan and purpose for your life. Jeremiah 29:11 says, "For I know the plans I have for you, declares the Lord, plans to prosper you and not to harm you, plans to give you hope and a future." Just know you are not a mistake and God doesn't make accidents. People might mess up, but God can use our mess-ups for his beautiful masterpieces.

12. Focus on Others – When we are constantly thinking about ourselves, we can get very dizzy. Rather than thinking about ourselves, let's think about others. How can I be a blessing to someone in need? When you are a blessing, you too will be blessed (Proverbs 11:25).

13. Think on Good Things – The Bible says to dwell on whatever is pure, true, noble, praiseworthy, and of a good report – (Philippians 4:8). We need to stop watching so much bad news and start reading the good news - The Bible. Start saying out loud and thinking good things about yourself. We also need to be careful of what we say about others. It's important to think and say good things about His children. The Bible says not to allow an evil word to come out of your mouth – (Ephesians 4:29). It's so important to look for the good in yourself and others. You will begin to have a new perspective.

14. Fight Back! - As you submit, surrender your life to God, He will give you the tools to fight back with and win! The Bible says, "Submit to God; Resist the devil and he Will flee" (James 4:7). You can fight back the devil with the word of God and in Jesus Name. God's Truth Sets People Free!

CONCLUSION

When I was an atheist, I was sure that there was no true evidence of God. But after learning about how much God did in people's lives, I can't deny Him any longer. Ever since I came into a working relationship with Jesus, it has enlightened my life, my mind, and ultimately my heart. Did you know you can experience this too? The Bible is very clear that God loves you so much that He is desperately seeking a reconciled relationship with you. Jesus even died for you, to get you back. There is nothing else God wants more than for you to encounter Him on a daily basis.

Many people are wondering how to encounter God. Some think it is a special formula or based on their own merit, but really it's neither.

Recognize you are not perfect. In fact, none of us are perfect! We can't obtain a relationship with Jesus by being good. Heaven isn't filled with good people. It is filled with people who recognized they were sinners and needed a Savior to save them. When you recognize you can't do it on your own and that you are not perfect; you are in a good place to receive His forgiveness. Jesus is called the lamb of God. He made the ultimate sacrifice for the entire world. Though He didn't deserve to die, He chose to die for you and me in order that our sins would be forgiven. We can be reconciled to God now. He loves us that much. Just call out to Jesus, admit your sins and ask for His forgiveness.

Encountering God isn't just to get to Heaven. Having a loving relationship with the Lord helps us with every facet of our daily life here on Earth. After you ask for forgiveness, then ask Jesus to come into your heart and make Him Lord of your life. He will make all things new. "I am the way, the truth, and the life. No one comes to the Father except through Me" (John 14:6).

Realize that God Loves you and wants a daily relationship with you. He will always be with you. Just like any other relationship, we need to spend time with that person.

The Bible is The Living Word of God. When you read it God will speak to you through it. "For the word of God *is* living and powerful, and sharper than any two-edged sword, piercing even to the division of soul and spirit, and of joints and marrow, and is a discerner of the thoughts and intents of the heart" (Hebrews 4:12).

Singing to The Lord, honoring and worshipping Him brings us into His presence. Also, getting into a good bible believing church is so important for your spiritual growth.

ADDITIONAL INFORMATION AND RESOURCES

Awakening The Nations – www.awakeningthenations.com Prayer line 866.480.4477

Real Life Radio Show – realliferadioshow.podbean.com

BelieverZ N da hood – www.believerzndahood.com

Reasons for Jesus – www.reasonsforjesus.com

http://cgi.org/ufos-exist-but-what-are-they/

http://www.godandscience.org/doctrine/astrology.html

http://pediaa.com/difference-between-astronomy-and-astrology/

www.gotquestion.org

Abortion Alternative – www.bethany.org/pregnancy-help - 800.238.4269

National Suicide Prevention – 800.273.8255

www.kristinaglackin.com

www.internationalhelpline.org

www.BeyondTheBandaide.com

www.jmgpenservices.com

www.northgatecounselinggroup.com

rick.malone@yahoo.com - 305.519.3386

jwteenchallenge@gmail.com

www.ingramcontent.com/pod-product-compliance
Lightning Source LLC
LaVergne TN
LVHW052254070426
835507LV00035B/2894